Developing and Localizing International Software

Hewlett-Packard Professional Books

Madell, Parsons, Abegg	*Developing and Localizing International Software*
Poniatowski	*The HP-UX System Administrator's "How To" Book*

Developing and Localizing International Software

Tom Madell
Clark Parsons
John Abegg
Hewlett-Packard Company

P T R Prentice Hall
Englewood Cliffs, New Jersey 07632

Library of Congress Cataloging-in-Publication Data

Madell, Tom.
Developing and localizing international software / Tom Madell,
Clark Parsons, John Abegg.
p. cm, -- (Hewlett-Packard professional books)
Includes index.
ISBN 0-13-300674-3
1. Computer software--Development. I. Parsons, Clark.
II. Abegg, John. III. Title. IV. Series
QA76.76.D47M34 1994 93-41466
005.1--dc20 CIP

Editorial/production supervision: *Dit Mosco*
Cover design: *Tommyboy Graphics*
Cover photo: *Masterfile* © Imtek Imagineering
Manufacturing buyer: *Alexis Heydt*
Acquisitions editor: *Karen Gettman*

Published by P T R Prentice Hall
Prentice-Hall, Inc.
A Paramount Communications Company
Englewood Cliffs, New Jersey 07632

The publisher offers discounts on this book when ordered in bulk quantities. For more information, contact:

Corporate Sales Department
PTR Prentice Hall
113 Sylvan Avenue
Englewood Cliffs, NJ 07632

Phone: 201-592-2863
Fax: 201-592-2249

Printed in the United States of America
10 9 8 7 6 5 4 3 2 1

ISBN 0-13-300674-3

Prentice-Hall International (UK) Limited, *London*
Prentice-Hall of Australia Pty. Limited, *Sydney*
Prentice-Hall Canada Inc., *Toronto*
Prentice-Hall Hispanoamericana, S.A., *Mexico*
Prentice-Hall of India Private Limited, *New Delhi*
Prentice-Hall of Japan, Inc., *Tokyo*
Simon & Schuster Asia Pte. Ltd., *Singapore*
Editora Prentice-Hall do Brasil, Ltda., *Rio de Janeiro*

Contents

Figures

Tables

Preface

In this book, we attempt to address the problem of how to get software to "behave" in a manner that will be equally relevant to diverse users throughout the world. The information presented shows both how to create international software and how to adapt such software to the particular language and display conventions found in a given region of the world. To answer these needs, we have endeavored to create a readable guide for those wishing to *learn* about software internationalization and localization. Foremost, however, the book is designed to offer task-focused and reference material for those who want to *use* such information.

This type of information will be of upmost importance to application developers who need the tools necessary to compete effectively in the international arena. However, even after software has been internationalized for use in a variety of countries, it typically cannot be used "as is"; non-programmers, such as translators, localizers, and system administrators must also perform certain tasks which enable the software to take on the proper appearance required by the language and cultural setting. These latter tasks are also described in this book. Finally, end-users of such international software also need to be aware of the various modifiable features contained within applications or within the operating system. Equipped with such knowledge, they will be able to, if necessary, either adjust such features themselves, or, recognize when they will need to request help to do so. This book is intended as a useful resource for anyone falling within the above groups.

Because *Developing and Localizing International Software* was written in the United States, the examples tend to focus on creating or adapting software for users whose language or culture is other than American English. The information presented is equally valid for developing software outside of the U.S. and for localizing software for use anywhere (including localizing non-English-based software for use in the U.S.)

The information presented is geared primarily toward use on UNIX-based systems. As a result, we have assumed some knowledge of the UNIX operating system in order for the reader to get the full flavor of the examples. The C programming language is heavily utilized within the UNIX development environment; consequently, the examples also assume C language familiarity. In spite of this, readers who wish to apply the information presented to non-UNIX systems should still be able to extrapolate overall internationalization and localization principles, although obviously not specific tools or examples.

Although some of the information and most examples were developed from *Native Language Support: User's Guide*, a manual for users of HP 9000 computers from Hewlett-Packard, most of the original material has been updated and extensively reorganized so that it more closely conforms to UNIX industry standards for internationalization. Additional information and examples are provided for users of HP 9000 systems, running HP's implementation of UNIX, HP-UX. All HP-UX-specific information is clearly identified as such within the text.

With the exception of the first two chapters which are intended to introduce the subject matter, the major objective of the remainder of the book is to enable the reader to perform necessary tasks. Referring to the different audiences described above, Chapters 4 and 5 should be of most interest to software developers, while Chapters 3, 6, and 7 will most meet the needs of localizers, system administrators, software translators, and end-users of international software.

The following is a chapter-by-chapter look at the contents:

Chapter 1, Introduction, presents background information and discusses fundamental concepts that are used throughout the book. It also provides a basic model for internationalized applications.

Chapter 2, Understanding Internationalization, provides necessary details on internationalization issues that must be addressed by developers, and to some extent, by software localizers. These issues include the complex topic of handling character sets and multi-byte character representations, dealing with local customs and conventions, and the display of local interfaces and messages.

Chapter 3, Running Internationalized Software, contains information primarily of interest to end-users. Topics covered include setting your terminal, the role of environment variables in controlling internationalized features, resetting your language environment, and viewing internationalized messages.

Chapter 4, Developing Internationalized Software, is primarily addressed to programming issues. It includes the topics of initializing your program to use non-default languages, retrieving language- and culture-specific information into your program, and dealing with single-byte and multi-byte codesets as well as wide character data types. Also included is basic information on using message catalogs.

Chapter 5, Special Programming Topics, provides additional information on initialization issues and use of message catalogs. The topic of codeset conversion may be relevant to localizers as well as programmers. The information on processing of right-to-left languages is an example of a section that while providing HP-UX-specific information only, may be of some interest to readers using non-HP-UX systems as well.

Chapter 6, Localizing Internationalized Software, contains information on HP-UX-specific Native Language Support (NLS) installation and system administration issues as well as system non-specific information on localizing, translating, and converting between codesets.

Chapter 7, Creating a New Language Environment, shows the steps that can be followed, when necessary, to modify or create localized files containing language- and culture-specific information.

Appendix A, Internationalization Routines and Commands, provides a quick reference to UNIX-standard internationalization routines and commands as well as HP-UX proprietary internationalization routines and commands.

Appendix B, Obsolete HP-UX Routines and Interfaces, is HP-UX-specific, showing both obsolete programming calls and tools and the recommended replacements.

Appendix C, HP-UX Languages and Codesets, is also provided as an HP-UX-specific reference.

The **Glossary** provides a convenient "look-up" for important terms. The terms are defined as used within the context of the book.

Acknowledgements

We would like to acknowledge the following individuals without whose efforts this book would not have been possible:

Janice Gee
Arne Thormodsen
Judy Chen
Mitsu Fujii

Jim Stratton
Ashok Waran
Carolyn Godfrey

We would also like to thank Patricia Matsoukas and Jim Heaton. Patricia wrote the original version of the *Native Language Support: User's Guide*, the Hewlett-Packard manual upon which this book was based. Jim updated the manual for two HP-UX releases in its early life.

About the Authors

Tom Madell is a Learning Products Engineer at Hewlett-Packard. He has a Master's degree in Psychology from the University of Michigan, a Ph.D. in Education from the University of Illinois, Urbana-Champaign, and has completed numerous programming and computer science courses. Prior to entering the computer field, he taught at the University of California, Davis and Illinois State University, among other institutions. More recently, he spent two years supporting end-users in a computing center environment at the University of Nevada. For the last six years, he has worked documenting operating systems, languages, and applications. He has written/updated two related manuals for HP: *Localizing and Customizing System Information* (MPE XL) and the *HP-UX Portability Guide*. During his career, he has also written a number of articles published in national scientific/professional journals.

Clark Parsons is a Learning Products Engineer at Hewlett-Packard. He has been involved in the design of documentation and computer-based tutorials over the past six years. Most of this work has been for HP's UNIX operating system (HP-UX) and related applications. Altogether, he has been with Hewlett-Packard for 20 years. He has a Master's degree in Educational Technology from the University of Northern Colorado and is currently continuing with doctoral work there in the same field.

John Abegg is a Learning Products Manager at Hewlett-Packard. He is also involved in the design of documentation for HP's UNIX operating system (HP-UX) and supporting applications. He, too, has been with Hewlett-Packard for 20 years. Prior to working at Hewlett-Packard, John graduated from Metropolitan State College of Denver with a B.S. degree in Electronics Engineering Technology. He subsequently wrote operating and programming manuals for desktop computers. He then moved into technical support for desktop computer users, specializing in network support. For four years, he sold HP computers as a field engineer in the Englewood, Colorado sales office. As a marketing engineer, he provided product management support for workstations. For the past five years, he has managed a group of learning products engineers (engineer-writers). He has written over a dozen operating, programming, and user guides as well as co-authoring the book "The Ultimate Guide to the vi and ex Text Editors."

1

Introduction

What This Book Is About

The capability of computer users anywhere in the world to interact with their systems using their *own* local languages and cultural conventions can no longer be thought of as just desirable; it's closer to being a necessity. This is especially true for the development and marketing of software products that aim for high international acceptance.

Unfortunately, much existing software is still designed and programmed taking into consideration only the needs of users in the particular country or region where it was developed.

Typically as a result, *either*:

- non-natives of this region are forced to struggle with foreign language and cultural representations in order to use the software in their home environment, *or*:
- software designers or engineers must re-design and re-compile the software to create a new version for *each* unique language and local environment that uses it.

Obviously, neither of these alternatives is desirable in terms of time, effort, or satisfaction level. A better approach is needed.

The purpose of this book is to show how to escape from this dilemma by enhancing the operating environment in a way that can support a variety of languages and cultures to the benefit of both users and systems/application developers. What will be described is a way of modifying the system-level and programming environment so that each can more closely match the many different language and cultural requirements of its users.

Two processes that enhance software for worldwide use are internationalization and localization.

Internationalization

From the above description, one might be tempted to think that software developers can simply allow for the ready translation of program output from one language to another. But such an assumption would be very much incomplete.

Quite apart from facilitating translation, developers for a worldwide audience must enable computer systems to read and write in the user's native language, that is, to understand and display characters and symbols that may be far different from, say, the characters and symbols that make up the words you are reading in this book. Further, the computer system must be enabled to have the capability to process these characters and text according to the rules of the user's language. For example, what if the program is required to alphabetize a list in a language containing a thousand letters or characters instead of the 26 letters in the English language set?

Additionally, software to be used worldwide must provide the flexibility to modify output conventions to comply with any local requirements (e.g., currency or numeric data is often displayed differently from one region to another). And finally, as suggested above, such software should provide the *capability* to allow for the translation of interfaces, messages, and prompts without necessitating many different language versions of the software.

Internationalization then, by this definition, is the process of building in the potential for worldwide use of software as a result of the efforts of programmers or software designers during the development or modification process.

However extensive internationalization efforts may be, internationalization alone is not sufficient to ensure that software will be usable at a particular locale or site. Localization, too, is usually necessary.

Localization

While internationalization is usually a process performed where and when the code is developed, localization is most often carried out subsequent to development, often in the location requiring the modifications. **Localization** is the process of actually adapting the potentially useful internationalized software to meet the needs of one or more users in a particular geographical area. It includes not only the translation of messages but also the selection or creation of the appropriate **language tables** containing the relevant local data for use on a given system. Localization activities are usually the function of users of internationalized software, system administrators, and software translators.

Internationalizing the UNIX Operating System

The UNIX operating system was conceived for use with terminals that generated 128 **ASCII** characters. Since the primary users were English-speaking Americans, the idea of internationalizing the operating system was initially not necessary.

However, as time passed, the UNIX operating system began to be used worldwide and eventually evolved into an industry-standard environment. As a result, a need developed to handle characters from other than the standard ASCII **codeset**, some of which contain as many as tens of thousands of characters. There was also the need to provide interfaces that allow users to interact with the operating system in their own language, rather than forcing them to understand American English messages and prompts.

The Hewlett-Packard Company answered these needs by creating **Native Language Support (NLS)**. NLS allowed the flexibility required to take into account a user's native language within the context of the overall UNIX operating system. NLS was subsequently adopted and further modified by **X/Open**, an organization committed to the implementation of open systems as part of an industry-wide and worldwide standard UNIX. (X/Open system requirements are published in the *X/Open Portability Guide*, the latest of which are collectively referred to as XPG4.)

Internationalizing Applications

Apart from the operating system, there was the need to internationalize applications run within the UNIX environment. Hewlett-Packard's NLS was also designed to create internationalized applications and to convert an existing single language program to allow it to have multi-language and multi-cultural capabilities.

Initially, internationalization only allowed for the support of **single-byte codesets**. However, since some Asian languages require more than a single byte to represent many characters, it became necessary for internationalization to add support for **multi-byte codesets**. The result was the development of the **Worldwide Portability Interfaces (WPI)** as defined by X/Open in XPG4. WPI is now generally the preferred approach for internationalization, especially for new development.

In order to internationalize a program, developers no longer need to deal with character data in a language-sensitive way, nor do they need knowledge of any foreign language. They do not even need to be aware of the ways different languages and codesets can vary. This makes the programming effort easier and provides for consistent treatment across languages. This is because of the development of **wide character** data types. Wide characters are now the standard way to represent multi-byte data during run time or processing time, regardless of the complexity of the character set being used.

As a result of these developments, the language capabilities of a program can now "transcend" the programmer's own linguistic knowledge, allowing the program to take on an appropriate appearance in many different local environments:

- Screens, prompts, and error messages are displayed in the user's language.
- Data is processed according to the varying requirements of the user's language.
- This is accomplished without re-creating and re-compiling source code. Translators are necessary, however, to create external messages to interface with the program. Language configurations must also be installed on the system; these are referenced at run time, specifying language-specific information and local conventions.

Features of an Internationalized Program

What features should an internationalized program include? Table 1-1 contrasts a typical American English, non-internationalized application with an otherwise identical but internationalized software program. The features summarized in Table 1-1 will be elaborated on throughout the remainder of this book.

Table 1-1.
A Comparison of an American English Program with an Internationalized Version

Non-Internationalized Program	Internationalized Version
Uses single-byte ASCII coded character set only.	Supports a variety of single- and multi-byte codesets necessary for the languages of international users. For example, **ISO 8859-1** for Western European users, **ISO 8859-2** for Eastern European users, and an encoding scheme called **Shift JIS** for Japanese users.
Source code must be altered and re-compiled to create new language-specific versions of the program because messages are hard-coded into the source code.	One discrete program is structured to support a variety of language environments. Translators without programming knowledge can alter program messages contained in a message file to create new language-specific versions; no alteration of source code is required because there are no hard-coded messages.
Data is manipulated according to rules of the American English language.	Data is manipulated according to rules of the user's native language.
Formats for expressing date, time, numeric, and monetary conventions are restricted to American English.	Formats for expressing date, time, numeric, and monetary conventions are modifiable to the user's culture-sensitive requirements.
Data is displayed on the screen in a left-to-right format.	Data can be displayed according to the text direction of the user's language.

How Are Internationalization Features Implemented?

In order to make internationalization feasible, the developer will need an extensive number of tools and routines to:

- ensure the correct handling of characters according to the rules of different languages and help preserve data integrity
- allow for the proper representation of local customs and conventions in software
- allow for interfaces and messages in local languages

Together, these tools and routines need to enable the creation of applications adapted for an end-user's needs regardless of the user's native language. The implementation must address not only a program's outward features such as the user interface, including displayed messages, user inputs, and output formats, but also the application's internal functions such as sorting and character handling.

An essential element of the internationalization model that evolved from Hewlett-Packard's NLS was the notion that it allow language-dependent features to be separated from the main program source code. As a result, the developer would be able to create a *single* internationalized application, a program that is capable of being extended into any number of localized, multi-language programs without the need for re-design or re-compilation.

An Internationalized Application

Our internationalizion model entails a simple premise: A discrete program will be empowered to "communciate" in a variety of languages. To accomplish this, an internationalized application can be designed best by subdividing it into three parts:

- *A Language-Independent Program*— Such a program achieves language sensitivity by a series of programmatic calls to each of the following modifiable, language-dependent components of the application.
- *Message Catalogs*— Rather than hard-coding messages such as prompts and error messages within the program itself, such messages are stored in external **message catalogs** with a different version for each supported language. For instance, instead of the program source code containing the statement:

```
printf ("display this string");
```

the program calls a routine that opens a specific message catalog for the desired language and another routine that retrieves the message.

- *Language Tables*— The third component of an internationalized application contains all language-specific processing information and conventions unique to a particular locale such as how characters are sorted and how output (such as numbers, times, and dates) is formatted. At run time, the program selects or "binds" a specific language table according to settings controlled by the user, the application developer, or the system administrator.

These three components of an internationalized application are depicted in Figure 1-1. Details of programmatic calls are explained in Chapter 4.

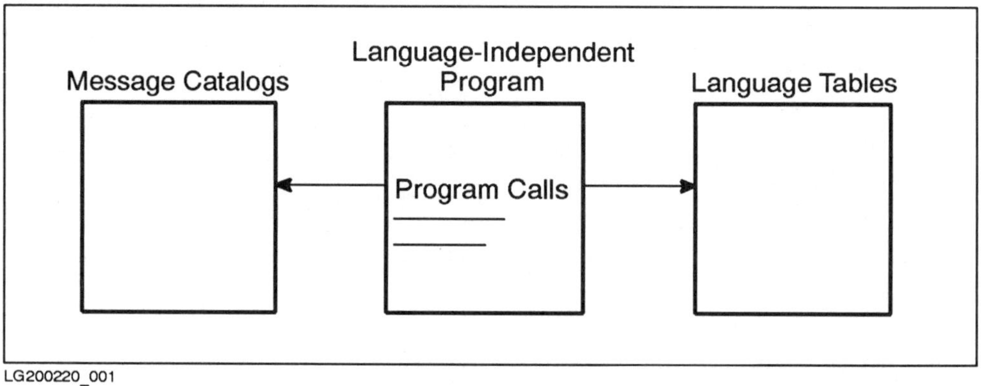

Figure 1-1. A Model for Internationalized Applications

In subsequent chapters, the term **locale** will be used to refer to the language table component of an internationalized application.

A Recap: Internationalization Advantages

To summarize, there are several unique advantages to the internationalization strategy presented here:

- Software need not be re-coded in different versions for different languages in order to localize it. As a result, only one version needs to be updated and maintained as well as manufactured, stocked, and shipped.
- Because all language-dependent information is kept external to the program source, neither programmers nor translators need to modify the program source in order to localize program language behavior. As a result, the possibility of introducing "bugs" during localization into the software is eliminated. And, instead of having to work with a huge amount of source code, translators can work from a discrete messages file containing only the text to translate. This frees them from the need to have programming skills.
- Since software can be localized more easily and inexpensively, such software should become more readily available and, as a result, fewer end-users will be forced to deal with difficult foreign representations.
- Several users can simultaneously work from the same program, with each able to specify a different set of language requirements.
- Using external language tables consolidates the structural and processing rules of each language into one physical location which can be modified to meet even more specific local requirements. And once installed, such tables will support any other internationalized program on the system.

Internationalization Standards

The majority of the material presented in this book adheres to X/Open XPG4 and **POSIX** (POSIX.1 and POSIX.2) standards for internationalization. For some of the material, however, the techniques described are HP proprietary and therefore available only on systems running **HP-UX**, Hewlett-Packard's implementation of UNIX. Such HP-specific material is clearly identified within the text. If portability of programs between various UNIX implementations is required, an applications developer should focus on the standards-conforming material. If the reader is an HP-UX user, or perhaps just especially interested in HP's implementation of internationalization, he or she will also want to review the HP-specific material.

Note The HP-specific material presented in this book is based on the 9.0 version of HP-UX and is current as of the date of this writing. If you are an HP-UX user and your system is 10.0 or later, you will need to contact your local HP sales office to inquire as to whether any additional documentation is available.

2

Understanding Internationalization

In Chapter 1, the following features of internationalization, each of which is included within standards-conforming UNIX system software, were introduced:

- character handling and preservation of data integrity
- local customs and conventions
- local interfaces and messages

This chapter discusses each internationalization feature in greater detail, as well as several other variations. The implementation of these features for developing and localizing internationalized software is presented in later chapters.

Character Handling and Preservation of Data Integrity

Internationalization provides the capability to identify, manipulate, and process text and characters in accordance with language-specific rules and to prevent data corruption.

Character Sets

In the UNIX environment, the default local language character set or codeset is usually **7-bit** ASCII (or USASCII). ASCII allows for the representation of 128 characters, sufficient for use with American English. All POSIX-compliant UNIX systems support this character set, which is also known as the POSIX portable character set.

It should be noted, however, that 7-bit ASCII is not sufficient to span the Latin-based alphabet used in many European languages. Likewise, for many

Asian languages, character sets can contain tens of thousands of characters. This is more than can be encoded in a **single byte** (7- or 8-bit), which is the conventional unit of storage used to represent character data. Thus, there are many implementations of non-ASCII character sets currently in use around the world.

For this and other reasons, internationalized character handling has adopted the following characteristics:

- The eighth bit of a character byte is never stripped or modified, as is sometimes done with the ASCII codeset.
- This eighth bit provides support for languages that have additional characters, accented vowels, consonants with special forms, and special symbols.
- **Multi-byte** coded character sets must be used for character sets that contain more than 256 members.
- Internationalization permits users to define their own language tables (locales) and accompanying character handling properties. Refer to Chapter 7, "Creating a New Language Environment" for more information.

Eight-bit codesets provide support to international users who speak and write phonemic languages, where characters represent sounds. A single byte, however, is not sufficient to represent the symbols of users whose language is ideographic, that is where characters represent objects or ideas. For example, Traditional Chinese contains over 50,000 distinct ideographs, or symbols. To provide for these users, **encoding schemes** that support multi-byte characters were introduced.

As mentioned above, for alphabets of more than 256 characters, such as Traditional Chinese or Kanji (consisting of Japanese ideographs based on Chinese characters), multi-byte character codes are required. For such languages, several encoding schemes have been defined. Encoding schemes provide a set of rules for parsing a byte stream into a group of coded characters.

With the introduction of encoding schemes for multi-byte characters, a problem arose. Because users who read and write ideographics still need ASCII for communicating with the operating system and for backward compatibility, it is possible to have a data stream consisting of a mixture of one- and two-byte characters. The resulting problem is one of character interpretation: How can a program interpret characters correctly, distinguishing between single and multi-byte characters? A number of solutions to this problem are available.

Hewlett-Packard provides a proprietary encoding scheme as a solution. This is described shortly under "HP-UX Supported Encoding Schemes for Multi-Byte Characters." Another such solution is provided by **Extended UNIX Code (EUC)**, an encoding scheme defined by AT&T USO Pacific, Ltd. This scheme is used for data processing and storage and is a de facto standard encoding scheme for Asian multi-byte codesets.

The EUC encoding scheme provides a general template for defining codesets and interpreting a byte stream. EUC allows four distinct codesets (called CS0 through CS3) to co-exist in a byte stream by restricting the legal bit patterns for each set to a specific template. Under the EUC encoding scheme, ASCII characters are uniquely identified by a most significant bit of "0" and occupy CS0; the EUC template restricts the most significant bit of *all* non-ASCII characters to a "1," even the second byte of two-byte characters.

HP-UX Supported Single-Byte Character Sets

Hewlett-Packard's HP-UX operating system supports many single-byte character sets. These 8-bit codesets permit the processing of many Eastern and Western European, Middle Eastern, and Asian languages.

Every HP-supported coded character set is a superset of ASCII. The HP-supported **8-bit** coded character sets for Western European languages are **ROMAN8** (HP proprietary) and the standard ISO 8859-1. These 8-bit codesets support an additional 128 character codes beyond those of ASCII. While this extension of the ASCII character set meets the needs of Western European users, it is not large enough to support languages such as Arabic and Greek that have alphabets completely different from those used in Western Europe or the U.S. For these languages, other 8-bit codesets have been designed. For a complete listing, please refer to Appendix C, "HP-UX Languages and Codesets."

HP-UX Supported Encoding Schemes for Multi-Byte Characters

A group of 2-byte codesets were developed by Hewlett-Packard called **HP-15**. This encoding scheme adheres to a common definition for interpreting a byte stream. The codesets that adhere to the HP-15 definition use a set of bytes with the high bit set to differentiate between 8- and 16-bit data. If the high order bit is zero, then the byte represents a one-byte ASCII character. Otherwise, the current byte may represent the first byte of a two-byte character or a one-byte non-ASCII character. The correct interpretation is provided through system tables. Since the high order bit acts as a flag bit, only 15 bits remain for data. Hence, the term HP-15. The codesets which are defined under this scheme are used to represent Traditional Chinese, Simplified Chinese, Korean, and Japanese.

While this representation allows 8-bit data to be distinguished from multi-byte data, there is one restriction. A byte stream must be examined sequentially. For an "arbitrary" byte, it is not possible to tell if the byte represents a single-byte character or the second half of a two-byte character.

HP-UX has limited support for two-byte EUC encodings. Currently, HP-UX includes `japanese.euc` (also referred to as "UJIS"), a codeset that supports Japanese two-byte codesets (but not for CS3).

Finally, for input and output, Hewlett-Packard uses a multi-byte character encoding scheme called **HP-16**. HP-16 is a companion code to HP-15, and is used exclusively for data communication. This encoding is normally never encountered in an application, but is generated by certain device drivers. It should not be of any concern to application developers or to end-users.

UNICODE: A Universal Codeset

Recently, a new character set and encoding standard has been developed: **ISO 10646-1**. ISO 10646-1 encodes a set of characters large enough to support most modern languages as well as several specialized applications. This standard was developed by a cooperative effort between ISO members and the **UNICODE** consortium, which was working on a privately-defined universal character set at the time. As it is currently defined, ISO 10646-1 characters may be either two or four bytes, with the bytes taking on any value in the range 0-255. Only a subset of all possible codes have been assigned. This subset is referred to as the Basic Multilingual Plane (BMP) and can be used as a two-byte character set.

When so used, it is equivalent to UNICODE 1.1 produced by the UNICODE consortium.

ISO 10646-1 is able to encode a large number of characters in a two-byte space when used in combination with two techniques:

- The same code value is used to encode similar characters included in Chinese, Japanese and Korean standards. This is referred to as "CJK unified ideographs" or as the "Han unification."
- Some ISO 10646-1 codes are combined to produce a single displayed "character" which does not otherwise exist in the ISO 10646-1 set. This is referred to as "composite sequences."

While the use of these techniques somewhat complicates the handling of ISO 10646-1 characters, their use will allow for support of many languages within a two-byte set. That said, it should be noted, though, that future expansion of ISO 10646-1 may require use of four-byte codes.

Note HP is actively participating in the development of ISO 10646-1 and associated standards. ISO 10646-1 is not currently supported on HP-UX systems.

Case Shifting

With internationalization, case shifting (that is, **upshifting** and **downshifting**) of characters can be done according to the local conventions for the native language selected.

It should be noted that while the ISO 8859 and the HP-specific ROMAN8 coded character sets have uppercase and lowercase for most alphabetic characters, some coded character sets for Asian languages do not.

Some languages discard accents when characters are shifted to uppercase. For example, European French commonly discards accents in uppercase, while Canadian French does not.

In addition, characters can no longer be upshifted or downshifted as in ASCII by adding or subtracting a fixed offset.

Finally, if there is no representation of case in the user's language, as is true for ideographic languages such as Chinese, characters are not shifted at all.

Collating Sequence

Languages may vary regarding the rules for ordering or sorting characters or strings, that is, regarding the **collating sequence**. Some languages can even have more than one set of acceptable collation rules. For example, the ideographic characters of the Chinese language can be sorted according to:

- the numeric value of the character as represented in the coded character set
- the number of strokes required to represent the character
- the radical (root) of the character
- the pronunciation of the character

As a result of such differences, the order in which character strings are sorted becomes language-dependent. Additionally, a discrepancy may exist between a character's order within a character set and its true lexicographical (that is, dictionary) order.

The ASCII collation order, that is, ordering by numeric value of bytes which is the default for UNIX, although fast, cannot meet the accuracy requirements of English language dictionary sorting. This is because lexicographical order sorts "a" after "A" and before "B," whereas ASCII-based order sorts "a" after the entire set of uppercase letters. This situation becomes more complex in an internationalized program that has been structured to handle many different coded character sets.

Although collating sequences are unique to a particular language and/or region, UNIX uses the ASCII collating sequence as system default when no other local collating sequence information has been made available.

Table 2-1 shows an example of sorting the same list based on the default ASCII sorting method as compared to German lexicographical sorting.

Table 2-1. Sorting Example 1: Default (ASCII) vs. German

Sorted by ASCII rules	Sorted by German rules
Airplane	Airplane
Zebra	ähnlich
bird	bird
car	car
ähnlich	Zebra

The table shows that while "ä" *follows* "b" in the ASCII coded character set ordering, it is sorted *before* "b" when sorted according to German lexicographical order. This illustrates that sorting based on the collating sequence of one locale is inappropriate when developing internationalized software. Even *within* the subset of lowercase values, character set order may not coincide with lexicographical order.

In addition to specifying the ordering of individual characters, some languages designate that certain groups of characters should be clustered and treated as a single character.

Table 2-2 shows an example of sorting the same list based on the default ASCII sorting method as compared to Spanish sorting rules.

Table 2-2. Sorting Example 2: Default (ASCII) vs. Spanish

Sorted by ASCII rules	Sorted by Spanish rules
chaleco	cuna
cuna	chaleco
día	día
llava	loro
loro	llava
maíz	maíz

The word "llava" is sorted after "loro" and before "maíz," because in Spanish "ll" is treated as a single character that is sorted after "l" and before "m." Similarly, the "ch" in Spanish is treated as a single character to be sorted after "c" but before "d." So, two characters are paired and treated as a single character; this is referred to as a **two-to-one character code pair**.

Similarly, in some languages, a single character is expanded when sorting strings and treated as if it were really two characters; this is referred to as a **one-to-two character code pair**.

Table 2-3 shows an example of of sorting the same list based on the default ASCII sorting method as compared to German sorting rules.

Table 2-3. Sorting Example 3: Default (ASCII) vs. German

Sorted by ASCII rules	Sorted by German rules
Rosselenker	Rosselenker
Rostbratwurst	Roßhaar
Roßhaar	Rostbratwurst

The difference occurs because when sorting strings in German, the single character ß (the "sharp s"), is treated as if it were actually two characters, "ss."

Other examples of sorting differences between some languages:

- Certain characters such as "-" may be ignored when collating strings.
- An accented character may be sorted together with the same character without the accent mark. That is, the two are treated identically until the last pass of a multi-pass collation.

Data Integrity

To say that software preserves **data integrity** means that the software must allow users to input characters required for their native language without corrupting those characters. For example, if a program prompts an international user named Müller to enter his name, the program should neither convert the "ü" to another character (such as by upshifting to "O", with the name output as MOller) nor should it map the character to an undefined value (such that "M ller" appears).

Some practical suggestions for maintaining data integrity will be presented under "Guidelines for Creating Internationalized Programs" in Chapter 4.

Local Customs and Conventions

Internationalization facilities can handle a variety of aspects of written language that can vary from region to region. These characteristics of language are referred to as local customs and conventions. They include such things as:

- the representation of numbers (numeric formatting)
- the representation of currency units (monetary formatting)
- the display of time and dates

Refer to Chapters 4 and 5 for descriptions of the library routines used to handle these local customs.

Note It should be noted that information can be region-sensitive even when comparing otherwise highly similar languages. So, for instance, even though Great Britain, the United States, Canada, Australia, and New Zealand all speak the English language, there are different local customs for such aspects of their written languages as monetary formatting and the display of dates.

Numeric Formatting

In the written representation of numbers, each of the following features may depend on local custom:

- The symbol that is used to separate the integer portion of a number from the fractional portion (the so-called **radix character**). In American English, this character is a period. In other languages, it may be a different character.
- The thousands separator which sometimes serves to separate a number larger than three digits. In American English, this character is the comma. In other languages, it may be a different character.
- The convention for grouping digits. In American English, digits are grouped by three's. In other languages, digits may be grouped differently.

For example, in American English, the following is the representation of a number:

```
2,345.678
```

When the same number is written in French, it appears as follows:

```
2 345,678
```

Here, digits are still grouped by three's, but the thousands separator is a blank character while the radix symbol is a comma.

Monetary Formatting

Currency units are represented differently depending on language and region. Not only does the symbol for a currency unit vary, but so does its placement. That is, the symbol can precede a numeric value, follow it, or appear within it.

The following example shows the difference between how currency is represented in the United States and in France. Note that in the first case the currency symbol string precedes the amount, while in the latter case, it trails the amount:

```
US$2,345.67

2 345,67 FF
```

Display of Time

Time too is displayed according to local convention. An obvious difference between countries is whether a 24-hour or 12-hour clock is used.

Note On HP-UX, the system clock runs on Coordinated Universal Time (UTC). Corrections to local time zones consist of adding or subtracting whole or fractional hours from UTC.

Display of Days, Weeks, Months, and Years

Names for days of the week and months of the year vary by language, as do their abbreviations. When referring to a written date, custom dictates the ordering of the year, month, and day as well as the separating delimiters for their numeric representation.

For example, in American English, the date "October 7, 1991" is represented numerically as:

```
10/7/91
```

However, in the U.K., it would be represented as:

```
7/10/91
```

and in Germany as:

```
7.10.1991
```

Further, to designate years, some regions use seasonal, astronomical, or historical criteria, instead of using the Western Gregorian calendar system. For example, in Japan, the official calendar is based on the year of reign of the current Emperor.

Local Interfaces and Messages

Another important feature of internationalization entails the ability to customize interfaces and messages for different geographical areas. The placement of messages in message catalogs helps to ensure that messages will be accessible for the purposes of translating into other languages as necessary, as well as allowing for easy updating or modification by programmers.

At run time, local users of an internationalized program can choose the desired language for display of menus, prompts, error messages, and any other online text. And since messages are kept in catalogs separate from the source code, no re-compilation is necessary when the program is run with a different interface.

Clearly the use of translated message catalogs will necessitate that translators fully understand the semantics of all system and program messages in order to correctly convey them to the end-user.

For example, consider the following message in American English:

```
cannot read at directory
```

Suppose, the intended meaning of this message is to make reference to a *specific* directory named "`at`". But due to the inherent ambiguity of the the message, a translator might interpret it in either of two ways:

- This message could be interpreted incorrectly as "cannot read the directory," with the meaning of "`at`" modified by the translator to fit the context. So, in German, the message might be translated as:

  ```
  Kann das Verzeichnis nicht lesen.
  ```

- Or, the message could be interpreted correctly as "`at` directory not readable.", which is the intended meaning. If so, in German, the message might read:

  ```
  at Verzeichnis nicht lesbar.
  ```

To facilitate arriving at the correct translation, the definition of "`at`" as the name of a specific directory should be provided to the translator through the inclusion of a comment preceding the affected message within the message catalog. Additionally, the information can be noted in a "cookbook" accompanying the message catalog. More information on using a cookbook is presented under "Guidelines for Using Messaging" in Chapter 4.

The above example also illustrates that the developer should strive for clear, unambigious messages in order to prevent this kind of problem from occurring at all.

More information on the use of message catalogs and solving translation problems is presented in Chapters 4 and 6.

Other Language Variations

Regular Expressions

UNIX allows the specification of arbitrary character strings through the use of **regular expressions**. The syntax of regular expressions has been extended in UNIX to allow use with other character sets.

Here is one example of an internationalized regular expression:

```
h[[=e=]]lp
```

This matches the word "help" spelled with any variation of the letter "e" (for example, e, é, ë, è) as specified in an "equivalence class" for a particular locale.

The existing syntax of a range expression (e.g., "[a-z]") has not changed. However, its meaning has been extended to mean "match any collating element which falls between the two given collating elements based on the currently active collation sequence."

Note The level of multi-byte support for regular expressions varies among vendors.

Data Directionality on HP-UX

Data directionality refers to the direction that a language is read by its readers, and of greater consequence for software development, the direction text within that language needs to appear on the screen. For example, European languages are displayed from left-to-right. On the other hand, some Middle Eastern languages are read, and therefore must be displayed, from right-to-left. Finally, some languages may require that text be displayed as a mix of left-to-right and right-to-left. Refer to "Processing Right-to-Left Languages on HP-UX" in Chapter 5 for more information on how HP-UX allows for processing of these types of data.

Note Currently, no special provisions are made within HP-UX for top-to-bottom languages, such as Chinese. These are handled by a left-to-right display.

3

Running Internationalized Software

What This Chapter Includes

This chapter presents information and tasks you will need to know to successfully get started using internationalized software.

Topics discussed include:

- setting your terminal
- understanding your language environment
- finding out what your local language environment includes
- resetting your local language environment
- locating reference information for internationalized commands
- viewing internationalized messages
- testing for the correct language environment

Setting Your Terminal

Your terminal must be set properly before you can use internationalized software.

Begin by checking to ensure that your terminal is so configured to enable it to transmit and receive either 8-bit or multi-byte data. This is accomplished by setting your terminal to 8 data bits and no parity. (The eighth bit is important for all non-ASCII codesets, whether they are single- or multi-byte, so you must ensure that your terminal is not configured to strip it.) Additionally, if you are using terminal emulator software on a workstation or PC, it may be necessary to choose the proper font for the character set you wish to work with.

Your terminal should also be set so that data is not corrupted by system software that might otherwise attempt to interpret the eighth bit of a byte. For internationalized software, this bit will be needed as part of the character code. To disable such an interpretation, run:

```
stty -istrip -parity
```

For convenience, add this command to your `.profile` or `.login` file.

Understanding Your Language Environment

Upon logging on to your system, the specific language environment for the operating system or any particular program you run may have already been determined for you. This will be the case if any of the following are true:

1. Your system was delivered with a pre-configured or pre-installed internationalized environment.
2. Your system administrator explicitly selected a particular internationalized environment.
3. A given program was written such that it does not allow the user to select another internationalized environment. In such cases, the program's language environment is pre-defined for you by the application developer.

Even though case 1 or 2 may be true, you, as a user, will still have the capability of interacting with UNIX or an application using a different language environment. If case 3 is true, however, you will not be able to run the program in any other internationalized environment.

If no language environment has otherwise been selected, a default language environment will be in effect on POSIX compliant systems. This environment is referred to as the **C locale** (also called the POSIX locale). This environment is specified by POSIX standards and uses the POSIX-defined portable character set.

When adapting a system or program for international use, you can modify the default language environment by means of one or more environment variables. You do this by resetting these variables, which will be described shortly.

The language environment is defined by the environment variables shown in Table 3-1. By setting these variables, you indicate to the system your unique requirements for various internationalization features.

Table 3-1. Internationalization Environment Variables

Variable	Description
LC_ALL	Specifies the value of a locale and all its associated features as defined in its language tables. Setting the value of LC_ALL takes precedence over any value specified by LANG or any of the variables below that begin with LC_.
LANG	Also specifies the value of a locale and all its associated features as defined in its language tables and message catalogs. However, LANG has lower precedence than LC_ALL and any of the variables below that begin with LC_. It may used in conjunction with any of the LC_ variables to define an environment with more than one set of language characteristics.
LC_COLLATE	Specifies user language requirement for string collation.
LC_CTYPE	Specifies user language requirement for character classification and case conversion.
LC_MESSAGES	Specifies user language requirement for displayed messages and for affirmative and negative response expressions.
LC_MONETARY	Specifies user language requirement for currency symbol and monetary value format.
LC_NUMERIC	Specifies user language requirement for decimal number format.
LC_TIME	Specifies user language requirement for date and time format and the names of days and months.
NLSPATH	Specifies the search path for message catalogs.
LANGOPTS (HP-specific)	Specifies data directionality for right-to-left languages.

The specific locale names which may be used to specify the value of an environment variable are not standardized and therefore will vary from system to system.

Local system default values for international environment variables are usually determined and set by your system administrator. Upon logging in, your environment may be set to these values unless you specifically reset them as described in "Resetting Your Local Language Environment" shortly.

To examine the current values of all of your environment variables including the international variables, type:

```
env
```

If none of the international environment variables are set or if you are not sure what international environment you need, consult with your system administrator to determine the appropriate settings.

Listing the Contents of Your Local Language Environment

Information about what has been input into a local language environment for each of the environment variables is available through the `locale` command.

You can use the `locale` command to display information about the `C` locale or other available locales. Here are some examples that illustrate the use of `locale`. For more details, see the `man` page for `locale`.

For the following examples, we'll assume that `french` was set by the system administrator as the system default language environment on an HP-UX system. Since locale names are system dependent, the name for a French language locale might be something else on another system.

Note You should not assume that the names nor the specific languages represented by the locale names referred to in the remainder of this book (such as `french`, `english`, or `american`) will be available on any particular system. They are used here as examples and because they are valid locale names for HP-UX systems.

The following example displays all items in the LC_TIME category:

```
% locale -ck LC_TIME
LC_TIME
abday="Dim";"Lun";"Mar";"Mer";"Jeu";"Ven";"Sam"
day="Dimanche";"Lundi";"Mardi";"Mercredi";"Jeudi"; \
"Vendredi";"Samedi"
abmon="janv";"févr";"mars";"avr";"mai";"juin"; "juil"; \
"août";"sept";"oct";"nov";"déc"
mon="janvier";"février";"mars";"avril";"mai";"juin"; \
"juillet";"août";"septembre";"octobre";"novembre";"décembre"
d_t_fmt="%A %.1d %B %Y %H:%M:%S"
d_fmt="%A %.1d %B %Y"
t_fmt="%H:%M:%S"
am_pm="";""
t_fmt_ampm="%H:%M:%S"
year_unit=""
mon_unit=""
day_unit=""
hour_unit=""
min_unit=""
sec_unit=""
era_d_fmt=""
era=""
```

As you may have detected, all of the items listed have something to do with expressing and formatting units of time. Further information on the meaning of these items can be found under "LC_TIME Keywords" in Chapter 7.

This following example limits the display to the value for the mon item, the subcategory that lists the names of the months within the local language.

```
% locale -ck mon
LC_TIME
mon="janvier";"février";"mars";"avril";"mai";"juin"; \
"juillet";"août";"septembre";"octobre";"novembre";"décembre"
```

Finally, to display the values for `LANG` and the other environment variables beginning with `LC_`, use the `locale` command without any arguments.

```
% locale
LANG=french
LC_CTYPE="french"
LC_COLLATE="french"
LC_MONETARY="french"
LC_NUMERIC="french"
LC_TIME="french"
LC_MESSAGES="french"
LC_ALL=
```

Resetting Your Local Language Environment

If the local system default values are not suitable for your needs, you can adjust the international environment to the appropriate locale by resetting the environment variables.

In order to use a different local language environment, that locale must be installed on your system. To check for installed locales, enter the command `locale -a`. If the locale you wish to use is not listed as installed, have your system administrator install it.

Environment variables can be set or reset in your `.profile` or `.login` file so that your preferred environment will be set when you log in. Or, to set a variable for your current session only, you can assign a value to a variable at the command line.

For example, if you wish to set a French locale within the Bourne or Korn/POSIX shell, enter the following:

```
LANG=french ; export LANG
```

This is equivalent to the C shell command:

```
setenv LANG french
```

If you will be running applications that need an international environment different from the system default and different from your usual environment, you can create and run a shell script that sets the environment variables needed for the application.

For example, to run the command **prog** with an environment containing more than one set of language characteristics, that is, a multi-language environment, the following POSIX shell script might be used:

```
# !/bin/sh
# prog is your own particular application
# script to set multi-language environment for prog
LANG=english ; export LANG
LC_TIME=italian ; export LC_TIME
LC_MONETARY=german ; export LC_MONETARY
LC_NUMERIC=french ; export LC_NUMERIC
# run prog
prog file1 file2
```

You should note that if instead of using **LANG=english**, you had used **LC_ALL=english**, then the remaining environment variables settings would have been ignored since **LC_ALL** takes precedence over the other environment variables included.

Locating Reference Information for Internationalized HP-UX Commands

On HP-UX systems, you can determine the extent to which any command you intend to use has been internationalized by consulting the online **man** pages or the appropriate pages in the *HP-UX Reference* (HP Part No. B2355-90033 for the 9.0 version of HP-UX). The section "Environment Variables" under EXTERNAL INFLUENCES within each listing, indicates international environment variables that affect the behavior of a command and whether a command has been internationalized for messages.

For example, to see how LC_TIME affects the **date** command, run:

```
man date
```

If a command has been internationalized for messages, you will see a statement such as:

```
LANG determines the language in which messages are displayed.
```

Viewing Internationalized Messages

Even if a command has been internationalized for messages, you should not necessarily infer that the appropriate message catalogs for any particular language are *installed* on your system for any locale other than the system default. Only if the catalogs are installed can local messages be displayed when the command is run; if they are not, the system default messages will continue to be displayed. This is still true even if an appropriate locale has been set with the `LC_ALL` or `LANG` environment variable.

For example, once you have set your international environment to an appropriate locale, the `sort` command will correctly sort data according to the collation sequence for that language. Messages issued by `sort`, however, will be determined by the `C` locale, the default locale for the system, unless localized message catalogs are available and have been installed on the system.

See Chapter 6 for more information on how to localize and install message catalogs.

Testing Your Language Environment

The best way to make sure you are ready to use a reset language environment is to do a brief test, such as the one described below:

1. To see if your chosen locale is installed on your system, run `locale -a`. If the locale is not installed, have your system administrator load it.
2. Once your locale is installed, set `LC_ALL` or `LANG` to the installed locale.
3. Run the `date` command.
4. See if you get the date with the format and naming conventions of the specified locale.

5. Now test for the appropriate message catalog by entering:

   `cat` *file*

   where the name entered for *file* is deliberately non-existent.

6. See if you get a message in the language specified by `LC_ALL` or `LANG`. (This message should be the localized equivalent of the system default message `cannot open.`)

If you get results consistent with your selected locale, you should now be able to use internationalized commands without further action. If you do not get the expected results, check with your system administrator to verify that all the required language-specific files are properly installed on the system.

Note If you find that `date` works according to the current setting of `LC_ALL` or `LANG`, but `cat` does not, this means that the message catalog for `cat` for the selected language has not been installed on your system. The `date` command relies on language tables and library routines, rather than message catalogs, so not having a message catalog installed for the selected language does not affect it.

4

Developing Internationalized Software

This chapter describes the programming steps necessary to create an internationalized application. Among the specific tasks discussed are:

- initializing local language information
- retrieving language-specific information
- handling characters
- using message catalogs for your applications

Initializing Local Language Information

In order to create a language-sensitive program, your program must request a specific language environment. Otherwise, the `C` locale will be used as the default environment. Likewise, users of your application can set a series of environmental variables according to their unique language requirements. However, this user language information is not made available to a program unless the program is initialized to retrieve it. Therefore, when you program international software, it is always necessary to provide the appropriate initialization which allows the program to retrieve the desired language information.

There are two elements that must be initialized in order to activate a program's internationalized behavior. These are:

- a locale for the program
- the program's messages

Two internationalization routines are used to provide the appropriate initialization:

- The locale for a program is initialized by calling `setlocale` to make locale information accessible to the program.
- Messages for a program are initialized by calling `catopen` to locate the appropriate messages and make them accessible to the program.

Setting Program Locale

To initialize your program's locale, you must supply two parameters to the `setlocale` routine:

`setlocale(`*category*`,` *locale*`)`

The *category* parameter specifies which variables within the program's internationalization environment you wish to set. The options you have for this parameter are outlined in Table 4-1.

Table 4-1. *category* **Arguments for** `setlocale`

category Option	Description
`LC_ALL`	Affects the behavior of all categories below.
`LC_COLLATE`	Affects the behavior of regular expressions and the internationalized string collation functions.
`LC_CTYPE`	Affects the behavior of regular expressions, character classification and conversion functions, and all routines which process multi-byte characters.
`LC_MESSAGES`	Affects the language in which messages are to be displayed as well as affirmative and negative response expressions.
`LC_MONETARY`	Affects the behavior of functions which handle monetary values.
`LC_NUMERIC`	Affects the handling of the radix character in the formatted input/output functions, the string conversion functions, and the other numeric formatting information.
`LC_TIME`	Affects the behavior of time conversion functions.

The *locale* parameter specifies the specific language table to use as a basis for the setting of the values for the selected *category*. To set the program's locale for the specified category, `setlocale` will accept the following arguments:

Table 4-2. *locale* **Arguments for** `setlocale`

Value	Description
"*locale name*"	If "*locale name*" is a valid locale, `setlocale` will set that part of the international environment associated with *category* as defined for that locale. A user's locale setting is therefore ignored.
`"C"` or `"POSIX"`	If the value of *locale* is set to `"C"` or `"POSIX"`, `setlocale` will set that part of the international environment associated with *category* as defined for the `C` locale. (The definition of the `C` locale is specified by X/Open and POSIX).
`""` (empty string)	If the value of *locale* is the empty string, the setting of that part of the international environment associated with *category* will depend on the current settings of the user's environment variables.
NULL	If the value of *locale* is NULL, `setlocale` queries the current international environment pertaining to *category*. It returns the user's current environment associated with *category*. You can then use the return string as the *locale* argument in a subsequent call to `setlocale`.

For example, the call:

```
setlocale(LC_ALL,"");
```

sets all categories of the program's locale to the values specified by the user's environment variables.

Activating Program Messages

Message catalogs allow program messages to be stored separately from the logic of the program, to be translated into different languages, and to be retrieved at run time, according to the language requirements of each user.

Information on creating message catalogs will be presented shortly under "Using Message Catalogs for Your Applications."

To allow your program to access a message catalog, use the **catopen** routine. This internationalization function opens the message catalog for reading and returns a message catalog file descriptor, **catd** of type **nl_catd**. (You will need to include **nl_types.h** at the beginning of your program to use **nl_catd**.)

Call **catopen** as follows:

```
catopen("name," oflag)
```

where:

name	is the program name enclosed in quotes; this indicates the name of the catalog to open. Or, the complete path name of the catalog can be specified. See note below.
oflag	should be set to NL_CAT_LOCALE. See note below.

If successful, **catopen** returns the message catalog file descriptor, **catd**. Otherwise, a value of (nl_cat)-1 is returned.

Note

It is stated above that you should use the program name as the *name* argument supplied to catopen. This will provide a generic descriptor of the message catalog to open. At run time, the program selects the particular message catalog supporting the user's language from the current setting of LC_MESSAGES provided in the setlocale call using the path(s) specified by environment variable NLSPATH. (More information on NLSPATH will be provided shortly.)

It is also stated above that you should set *oflag* to NL_CAT_LOCALE. If *oflag* is set to NL_CAT_LOCALE, the LC_MESSAGES *category* determines the message catalog to open. However, if you set *oflag* to 0, the LANG environment variable determines the message catalog to open.

Also note that the two initialization routines, setlocale and catopen, can be called independently, except if you set the *oflag* parameter to NL_CAT_LOCALE as recommended, in which case you *must* precede the call to catopen with a call to setlocale. The setlocale routine makes information from the appropriate language tables available. Your program can later reference this information to provide language-sensitive processing. In contrast, catopen opens a message catalog, and thus affects aspects of the user interface, rather than language-sensitive processing.

Recommended Initialization

As described above, setlocale and catopen should be used to initialize your program. For convenience, the following initialization code is recommended for most applications:

```
#include <nl_types.h>
    ⋮
nl_catd catd;
    ⋮
if ( !setlocale(LC_ALL, "") ) {
    fputs("setlocale failed,
       continuing with \"C\" locale.", stderr);
    putenv("LC_ALL="); /* to prevent future
                          setlocale calls from failing */
    catd = (nl_catd)-1;
    }
else
    catd = catopen("name", NL_CAT_LOCALE);
    ⋮
```

Figure 4-1 summarizes the processes discussed thus far.

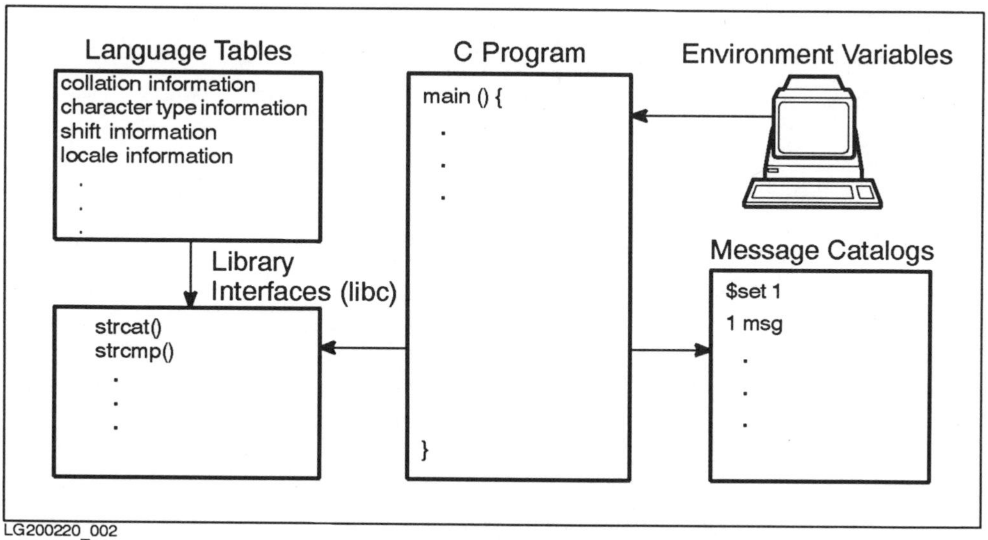

Figure 4-1. The Program Environment

Retrieving Language-Specific Information

Each supported language has an associated language table, called its locale, which contains information specific to a given geographic area. To retrieve this locale-specific information into your programs, use the `nl_langinfo` routine.

Note Access to information about the currently active locale is also available through `localeconv` (and `getlocale` on HP-UX systems.) The `localeconv` routine provides access to locale information that pertains to numeric formatting. On HP-UX, the `getlocale` routine provides access to `setlocale` status information. The `localeconv` routine is discussed shortly under "Handling Characters." Also see the `man` page for `localeconv` for more information.

To call `nl_langinfo`, you must supply a single parameter indicating the type of information you are requesting:

`nl_langinfo(`*type*`);`

The parameter *type* may be any of the categories shown in Table 4-3.

Table 4-3. Parameters Defined for `nl_langinfo`

Item	Description
`D_T_FMT`	Date and time format string appropriate for the current language.
`D_FMT`	Date format string appropriate for the current language.
`T_FMT`	Time format string appropriate for the current language.
`T_FMT_AMPM`	Appropriate time representation in the 12-hour clock format with `AM_STR` and `PM_STR`.
`AM_STR`	Equivalent symbols for a.m. (before noon). Used with 12-hour time.
`PM_STR`	Equivalent symbols for p.m. (afternoon).
`DAY_`*n*	The name of *n*th day of the week, where *n* ranges from `1` to `7`.
`ABDAY_`*n*	The abbreviated name for the *n*th day of the week, where *n* ranges from `1` to `7`.
`MON_`*n*	The name of the *n*th month in the Gregorian year, where *n* ranges from `1` to `12`.
`ABMON_`*n*	The abbreviated name of the *n*th month in the Gregorian year, where *n* ranges from `1` to `12`.
`ERA`	Emperor/Era description segments.
`ERA_D_FMT`	Default string for formatting the Emperor/Era name and year.
`ERA_D_T_FMT`	Default string for formatting the Emperor/Era time and date.
`ERA_T_FMT`	Default string for formatting the Emperor/Era time.
`RADIXCHAR`	Radix character ("decimal point" in English).
`THOUSEP`	Separator for thousands ("comma" in English).
`YESEXPR`	Affirmative response expression for yes/no questions.
`NOEXPR`	Negative response expression for yes/no questions.

Table 4-3. Parameters Defined for `nl_langinfo` (continued)

<table>
<tr><th>Item</th><th>Description</th></tr>
<tr><td><code>YESSTR</code></td><td>Affirmative response for yes/no questions. [Note that this item will be withdrawn in a future POSIX revision.]</td></tr>
<tr><td><code>NOSTR</code></td><td>Negative response for yes/no questions. [Note that this item will be withdrawn in a future POSIX revision.]</td></tr>
<tr><td><code>CRNCYSTR</code></td><td>Specifies the placement of the currency symbol. If <code>-</code> (minus), it precedes the monetary value, if <code>+</code>, it follows the monetary value, and if “.”, it replaces the radix symbol in the monetary value.</td></tr>
<tr><td><code>CODESET</code></td><td>Specifies the codeset name. Note: Not currently implemented on HP-UX.</td></tr>
<tr><td><code>ALT_DIGITS</code></td><td>Specifies alternative symbols for digits Note: Not currently implemented on HP-UX.</td></tr>
<tr><td><code>BYTES_CHAR</code>
(HP-specific)</td><td>Maximum number of bytes per character for the character set used to represent the language.</td></tr>
<tr><td><code>DIRECTION</code>
(HP-specific)</td><td>Value to indicate text direction. The values <code>null</code> and <code>0</code> indicate the characters are arranged from left-to-right within a line and lines are arranged from top-to-bottom. A value of <code>1</code> indicates characters are arranged from right-to-left within a line and lines are arranged from top-to-bottom.</td></tr>
<tr><td><code>ALT_DIGIT</code>
(HP-specific)</td><td>A string of characters that are mapped into the ASCII equivalent string <code>0123456789 +-.,eE</code>. A null value for the string indicates the language has no alternative digits.</td></tr>
<tr><td><code>ALT_PUNCT</code>
(HP-specific)</td><td>A string whose characters are mapped into the ASCII equivalent string <code>!"#%&()*+-./:;<=>?@[ ]^_‘{|}~</code> in <code>american</code> locale usage. A null value for the string indicates the language has no alternative punctuation characters.</td></tr>
<tr><td><code>YEAR_UNIT</code>
(HP-specific)</td><td>Symbol for years.</td></tr>
</table>

Table 4-3. Parameters Defined for `nl_langinfo` (continued)

Item	Description
`MON_UNIT` (HP-specific)	Symbol for month.
`DAY_UNIT` (HP-specific)	Symbol for day.
`HOUR_UNIT` (HP-specific)	Symbol for hours.
`MIN_UNIT` (HP-specific)	Symbol for minute.
`SEC_UNIT` (HP-specific)	Symbol for second.

Here is an example of using the **nl_langinfo** routine. The following code segment prints the days of the week for the current locale:

```
#include <nl_types.h>
#include <langinfo.h>
#include <stdio.h>
#include <locale.h>

void display_days()
{
   printf("%s\n", nl_langinfo(DAY_1));
   printf("%s\n", nl_langinfo(DAY_2));
   printf("%s\n", nl_langinfo(DAY_3));
   printf("%s\n", nl_langinfo(DAY_4));
   printf("%s\n", nl_langinfo(DAY_5));
   printf("%s\n", nl_langinfo(DAY_6));
   printf("%s\n", nl_langinfo(DAY_7));
}

main()
{
nl_catd catd;
if ( !setlocale(LC_ALL, "") ) {
    fputs("setlocale failed,
       continuing with \"C\" locale.", stderr);
    putenv("LC_ALL="); /* to prevent future
                               setlocale calls from failing */
    catd = (nl_catd)-1;
    }
else
    catd = catopen("%%name%%", NL_CAT_LOCALE);
display_days();
}
```

Note To view other locale-specific information, set the `LC_ALL` or `LANG` environment variable to different installed locales and re-run your program.

Handling Characters

This section provides information on:

- string processing and comparisons
- upshifting and downshifting characters
- identifying character types
- numeric formatting
- display of date and time
- monetary formatting
- character input and output
- formatting of input and output

If your application will *only* support single-byte languages and you are sure you will *not* support multi-byte languages, use the application interfaces described below under "Processing Characters Using the Traditional C Language Interfaces." If there is *even a possibility* that your application will eventually support multi-byte languages, consider using the application interfaces described later in the chapter under "Processing Using Wide Characters."

Processing Characters Using the Traditional C Language Interfaces

The C language interfaces were designed primarily for use with single-byte codesets, although some will work with multi-byte codesets as well.

String Processing and Comparisons

The C programming language includes a series of string handling routines. Table 4-4 lists routines for character and string processing along with a brief description of each. For more complete information, see your `man` pages.

Table 4-4. Routines for Character and String Processing

Routine	Description
`char *strcat`	Appends a copy of a second string to the end of a first string.
`char *strncat`	Same as **`strcat`** except appends at most *n* bytes.
`int strcmp`	Returns an integer greater than, equal to, or less than zero, according to whether the first string pointed to is greater than, equal to, or less than the second string pointed to, based on a character code value comparison.
`int strncmp`	Same as **`strcmp`** except examines at most *n* bytes.
`char *strcpy`	Copies a second string to a first string, stopping after the null byte has been copied.
`char *strncpy`	Same as **`strcpy`** except copies exactly *n* bytes.
`size_t strlen`	Returns the number of bytes in a string, not including the terminating null byte.
`char *strchr`	Returns a pointer to the first occurrence of a byte in a string, or a null pointer if the byte does not occur in the string.
`char *strrchr`	Returns a pointer to the last occurrence of a byte in a string, or a null pointer if the byte does not occur in the string.
`char *strpbrk`	Returns a pointer to the first occurrence in a string of any byte from a second string, or a null pointer if no byte from the second exists in the string.
`size_t strspn`	Returns the length of the maximum initial segment of a first string which consists entirely of bytes from a second string.
`size_t strcspn`	Returns the length of the maximum initial segment of a first string which consists entirely of bytes not from a second string.

Table 4-4.
Routines for Character and String Processing (continued)

Routine	Description
`char *strstr`	Returns a pointer to the first occurrence of a second string in a first string, or a null pointer if the second string does not occur in the first string.
`char *strtok`	Considers a string to consist of a sequence of zero or more text tokens separated by spans of one or more bytes from the separator string. The first call returns a pointer to the first byte of the first token, and writes a null byte into the string immediately following the returned token.
`int strcoll`	Compares its two arguments and returns an integer less than, equal to, or greater than zero, depending on whether the first is lexicographically less than, equal to, or greater than the second.
`size_t strxfrm`	Transforms the first string pointed to and places the resulting string into an array. Used in conjunction with `strcmp` for improved performance lexicographical collation.

With the exception of `strcmp`, `strcpy`, `strcat`, `strcoll` and `strxfrm`, which support single- and multi-byte character code sets, the routines listed in Table 4-4 only support single-byte character code sets. For expanded internationalized string processing, see "Processing Using Wide Characters."

Note

`strcmp` supports multi-byte characters only for comparisons for equality, not less than or greater than.

For some applications, in particular those in which many strings are compared against one constant string, you can improve performance by using `strxfrm` to convert strings to a form that can be compared using `strcmp`. (`strcmp` is generally faster than `strcoll`.) The following program illustrates this application. Error checking the conversion by `strxfrm` has been omitted:

```
char *s1, *s2, *t1, *t2;
int  n1, n2;
     ⋮
strxfrm(s1, t1, n1);
strxfrm(s2, t2, n2);
     ⋮
if ( strcmp(t1, t2) > 0 ) {
    /* == strcoll(s1, s2) */
     ⋮
```

Upshifting and Downshifting Characters

The C programming language provides the routines shown in Table 4-5 to upshift and downshift characters. Internationalization supports use of these routines for single-byte character code sets. For multi-byte character code sets, see "Processing Using Wide Characters." See your **man** pages for more information about this specific group of routines.

Table 4-5. Upshifting and Downshifting Routines

Routine	Description
toupper(*c*)	If *c* represents a valid lowercase letter for the current language, **toupper(*c*)** returns the integer character code of the upshifted value of *c*; otherwise **toupper(*c*)** returns *c* unaltered. The domain of this routine is **-1** to **255**
tolower(*c*)	If *c* represents a valid uppercase letter for the current language **tolower(*c*)** returns the integer character code of the downshifted value of *c*; otherwise, **tolower(*c*)** returns *c* unaltered. The domain of this routine is **-1** to **255**.
_toupper(*c*)	This macro performs like **toupper** but is faster and has a restricted domain of **0** to **255**. *c* must be a valid lower case character.
_tolower(*c*)	This macro performs like **tolower** but is faster and has a restricted domain of **0** to **255**. *c* must be a valid upper case character.

Identifying Character Types

Although non-internationalized ASCII versions of routines to classify characters have been a part of the standard C programming language for years, internationalization provides routines to classify characters according to the rules of any single-byte character code set. This assumes that a program has been initialized for local language information with `setlocale`.

All the routines included in Table 4-6 below return a non-zero integer if the indicated condition is true; otherwise they return `0`. For more information about these routines refer to your `man` pages.

Table 4-6. Character Identification Routines

Routine	Condition
`isalpha(`*c*`)`	Is *c* an alphabetic character?
`isupper(`*c*`)`	Is *c* an uppercase alphabetic character?
`islower(`*c*`)`	Is *c* a lowercase alphabetic character?
`isdigit(`*c*`)`	Is *c* a decimal digit?
`isxdigit(`*c*`)`	Is *c* a hexadecimal digit?
`isalnum(`*c*`)`	Is *c* an alphanumeric character?
`isspace(`*c*`)`	Is *c* a tab, new-line, space, or any character that creates "white space" in displayed text?
`ispunct(`*c*`)`	Is *c* a punctuation character?
`isprint(`*c*`)`	Is *c* a printing character?
`isgraph(`*c*`)`	Is *c* a character with a visible representation?
`iscntrl(`*c*`)`	Is *c* a control character?
`isascii(`*c*`)`	Is *c* an ASCII character?

Note Although the form of the internationalization character identification routines do not differ from the "ASCII only" routines, the type of argument passed cannot be `char`. When passing 8-bit bytes to these routines, the data should be `int` (or cast to it) to ensure correct sign extension.

Numeric Formatting

The numeric formatting routines below have been internationalized and give locale-sensitive results.

Table 4-7. Numeric Formatting Routines

Routine	Description
`strtod`	Converts a string to a `double`, correctly interpreting the radix character according to the currently active value of the `LC_NUMERIC` category.
`strtol`	Converts a string to a `long`
`strtoul`	Converts a string to an `unsigned long`.

Note The radix character is determined by the value of the `decimal_point` keyword in the `LC_NUMERIC` category. See Chapter 7 for more information.

Other Numeric Formatting

You can retrieve currency symbol and position information (as well as other numeric formatting conventions) through the `localeconv` internationalization library routine.

The following example illustrates how you can use the information returned by `localeconv` to allow for formatting of monetary values within an internationalized application.

The program prints a monetary value for the currently active locale. `localeconv` returns a structure containing locale-specific numeric formatting conventions. Two members of this structure are accessed:

`p_cs_precedes`
: Set to `1` if the currency symbol precedes a non-negative monetary quantity; otherwise set to `0`.

`n_cs_precedes`
: Set to `1` if the currency symbol precedes a negative monetary quantity; otherwise set to `0`.

For more information on `p_cs_precedes` and `n_cs_precedes`, refer to "LC_MONETARY Keywords" in Chapter 7.

```
#include <locale.h>
#include <stdio.h>
#include <stdlib.h>

main(argc, argv)
int argc;
char **argv;
{
   struct lconv *lconv_ptr;            /* pointer to structure returned by
                                          localeconv*/
   float  number;
   char   *cs_precedes, *cs_succeeds;  /* pointers for the preceding currency
                                          symbol and the succeeding currency
                                          symbol*/

   nl_catd catd;
   if ( !setlocale(LC_ALL, "") ) {
       fputs("setlocale failed,
          continuing with \"C\" locale.", stderr);
       putenv("LC_ALL="); /* to prevent future setlocale calls from failing */
       catd = (nl_catd)-1;
    }
   else
       catd = catopen("name", NL_CAT_LOCALE);
   lconv_ptr = localeconv();
   number = (float)atof(argv[1]);       /* convert string to a float */
```

```
    /* if the number is non-negative and the currency symbol precedes a
       non-negative formatted monetary quantity OR if the number is
       negative and the currency symbol succeeds a negative formatted
       monetary quantity, set the preceding currency symbol pointer to
       the currency symbol */

     if (number >= 0 && lconv_ptr->p_cs_precedes == 1 ||
        number < 0 && lconv_ptr->n_cs_precedes == 1 )   {

        cs_precedes = lconv_ptr->currency_symbol;
        cs_succeeds = "";
     }
     /* otherwise set the succeeding currency symbol to the currency symbol */

     else {
        cs_precedes = "";
        cs_succeeds = lconv_ptr->currency_symbol;
     }
     printf("%s %6.2f %s\n", cs_precedes, number, cs_succeeds);
}
```

Other information in the `lconv` structure shown in the above example describes decimal point, thousands separator, spaces used with the currency symbol, and other locale-specific formatting information.

Formatting of Date and Time

The `ctime` and `asctime` date and time routines always give `C` locale results. To get date and time information that reflects other locales, use `strftime`.

Table 4-8. Date and Time Formatting Routines

Routine	Description
`strftime`	Similiar to `ctime` but accepts an optional format string which should be placed in a message catalog.
`strptime`	Converts time string into values stored in the time structure.

Monetary Formatting

The internationalization of monetary formatting is more complicated than numeric formatting because in some countries the currency symbol is placed before the amount, while in others, it is placed within or after the amount. To get locale-sensitive information, use the routine below.

Table 4-9. Monetary Formatting Routine

Routine	Description
`strfmon`	Convert a monetary value to a string using currency information within the current locale.

Character Input and Output

The C programming language includes character input and output routines. These routines are designed for use with single-byte characters. Although they may be used for multi-byte input and output in certain cases, it is generally recommended that the programmer use the Worldwide Portability Interfaces discussed shortly if multi-byte input and output is needed.

Table 4-10 lists routines for character input and output along with a brief description of each. For more complete information, see your `man` pages.

Table 4-10. Routines for Character Input and Output

Routine	Description
`int getc`	Reads a character from input and converts it to an integer.
`int getchar`	Same as `getc(stdin)`.
`int fgetc`	Same as `getc()`, but is a function rather than a macro.
`char *gets`	Reads characters from standard input into an array.
`char *fgets`	Reads characters from input into an array.
`int putc`	Writes a character to output.
`int putchar`	Same as `putc(stdout)`.
`int fputc`	Same as `putc()`, but is a function rather than a macro.
`int puts`	Writes a string to standard output.
`int fputs`	Writes a string to output.
`int ungetc`	Inserts a character into an input stream.

Formatting of Input and Output

In addition to the usual formatting capabilities for input and output strings and numeric values, printing and scanning functions were modified to provide a flexible formatting feature for international applications. The flexible formatting feature enables you to read and write order-sensitive information to reflect different local conventions. Examples of such order-sensitive information include:

- the relative position of day and month in the date
- the position of the currency symbol
- the radix symbol

Printing Formatted Output. The conversion character, `%`, can be replaced with the sequence `%`*n*`$`, where *n* is a decimal digit in the range `1` to `9`, specifying the argument you want the conversion to be applied to. For example, if `string1 = "friend"` and `string2 = "hello"`, then `printf` will work as follows:

Statement:	`printf("%2$s%1$s.", string1, string2);`
Result:	`hello friend.`

By using this flexible formatting feature in combination with a message catalog specifying the order required, output appropriate to a given geographic region can be created.

For example, to print a locale-specific version of the date, include the following statement in your program:

```
printf((catgets(nlmsg,NL_SET,3,"%1$d%2$d/%3$d")), month,day,yr)
```

To handle the differences in conventions, each regional message catalog needs to contain the required formatting information. Thus, an `american` message catalog might contain the following formatting string to correctly print the date:

```
1 The date is: %1$d/%2$d/%3$d
```

A `german` catalog, however, might contain:

```
1 Heute ist: %2$d.%1$d.%3$d
```

Suppose `month = 1` (Jan.), `day = 25`, and `year = 93` (1993).

If `LANG=american`, then the following will be printed:

```
1/25/93
```

If, however, `LANG=german`, then the following will be printed:

```
25.1.93
```

For a more complex example, consider the following code:

```
#include <nl_types.h>
#include <stdio.h>
#include <locale.h>

main(){
nl_catd nlmsg_fd;
int month, day, year, num_read;

setlocale(LC_ALL,"");
nlmsg_fd=catopen("birthday",NL_CAT_LOCALE);

printf(catgets(nlmsg_fd,NL_SETN,2,"Please enter your birthday (in the form MM/DD/YY\n)"));
num_read=nl_scanf(catgets(nlmsg_fd,NL_SETN,3,"%1$d/%2$d/%d$d"),&month,&day,&year);
printf(catgets(nlmsg_fd,NL_SETN,4,"month=%1$d\n day=%2$d\n year=19%3$d\n\n"),month,day,year);
}
```

Figure 4-2 shows sample content of American and German message catalogs and the resulting user interface.

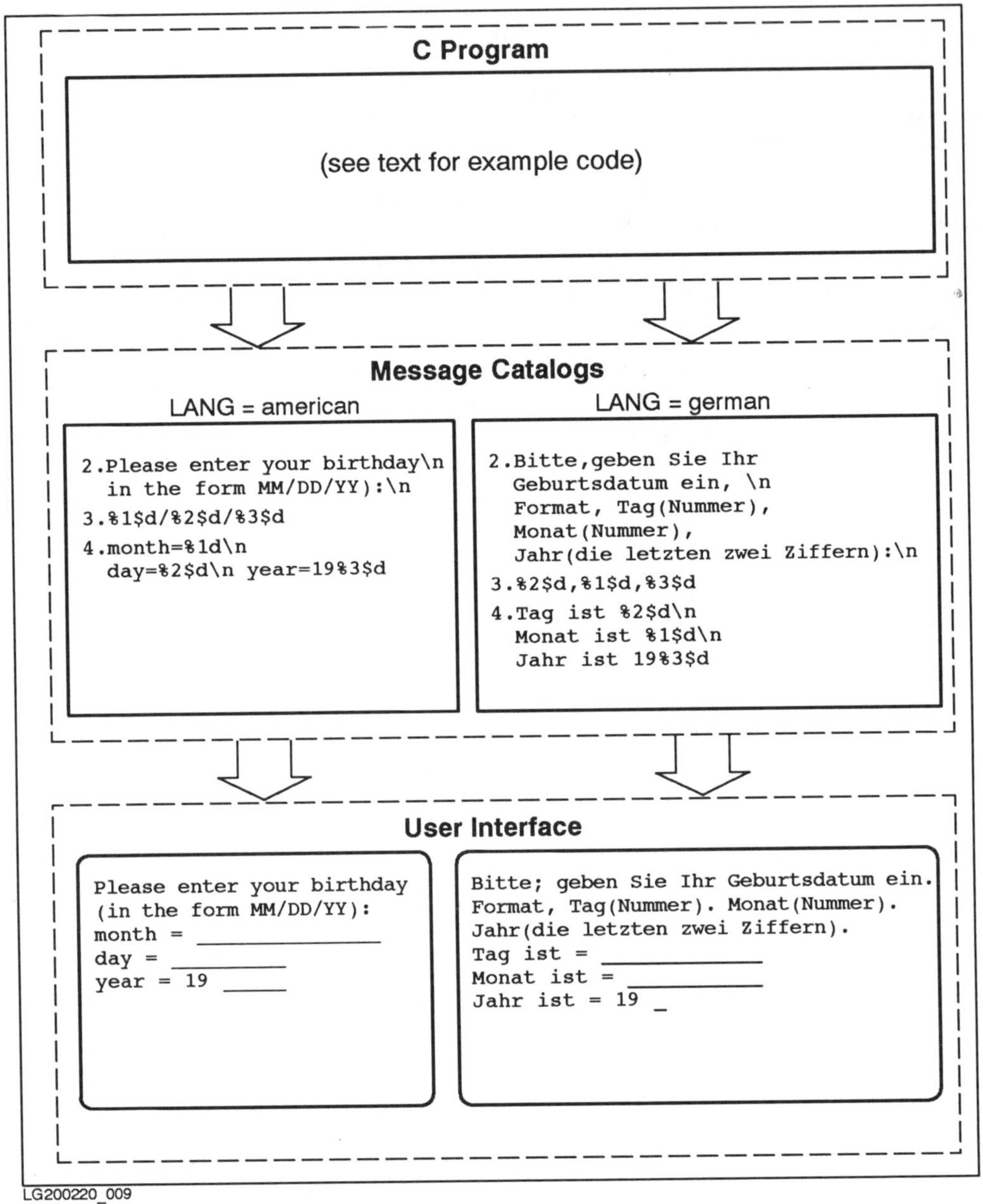

Figure 4-2. Printing Formatted Output

Note	If `catopen` fails to open the message catalog during program initialization, the default string included in the call to `catgets` is used.

The following print routines also support the international flexible formatting feature:

`fprintf(`*stream, format [arg list]*`)`
`sprintf(`*s, format [arg list]*`)`
`vfprintf()`
`vprintf()`
`vsprintf()`

Reading Formatted Input. The flexible formatting feature also applies to the read routines. The conversion character, `%`, is replaced by the sequence `%`*n*`$`, where *n* is in the range `1` to `9`. The conversion is applied to the *n*th argument rather than the next unused one.

The following read routines support the international flexible formatting feature:

`scanf(`*format* `[,` *pointer*`]...)`
`fscanf(`*stream*`,` *format* `[,` *pointer*`]...)`
`sscan(`*s*`,` *format* `[,` *pointer*`]...)`

Processing Using Wide Characters

The original approach to internationalization required a program to process multi-byte data in non-standard ways, in accordance with the particular codeset being used. This contrasts to the currently available wide character approach which uses the Worldwide Portability Interfaces (WPI) to process language-dependent data. Wide character encoding enables a program to deal with data in a standard way regardless of codeset. Multi-byte characters are represented as wide, constant width characters.

WPI allows you to convert data to and from its internal coding in wide characters, keeping you from having to know the details about large character sets in which one character may consist of several bytes. The wide character representation is simpler and more convenient because it offers a single data type for all codesets.

Wide character representations are specified by X/Open and supported by multiple vendors and therefore allow for portable applications. However, the use of larger buffers to support wide characters in place of one-byte characters can cause performance decreases and may increase memory consumption.

The wide character approach to internationalizing applications is usually the preferred approach for supporting characters consisting of multiple bytes.

Guidelines for Using Wide Characters

The need for and process of converting from non-internationalized programs to WPI must be considered on a program by program basis. You should limit your usage of WPI to avoid performance degradation and possible memory consumption increase.

You only need to use wide characters when doing character manipulation or character scanning. In these situations, dealing with fixed width, wide characters simplifies processing. This is because without wide characters, programs would need to know the starting byte and ending byte of each multi-byte character. Such a task is complex since individual bytes of a multi-byte character may appear to be a single byte if seen out of context.

Changing to Wide Characters

A set of routines is available to convert between multi-byte characters and wide characters. These routines are presented in Table 4-11.

Use the following steps to convert an existing program to WPI:

Step 1. Identify areas of character manipulation and character scanning.
Step 2. Convert `char` data types to `wchar_t` in the areas identified.
Step 3. Find calls to routines which may require change; where parallel routines exist, change non-WPI calls to the equivalent WPI versions. For example:

Instead of this	Use this
`strcmp`	`wcscmp`
`isdigit`	`iswdigit`
`fgetc`	`fgetwc`

Step 4. In cases where no parallel routine exists, you need to add code to convert wide character data to multi-byte data. (e.g., use `wcstombs`, as described in Table 4-11.)
Step 5. Finally, pass multi-byte data to "standard" routines.

For sample code showing the use of WPI, see "Examples Comparing Single-Byte Interfaces and WPI" shortly.

Multi-Byte Character and String Conversions

For multi-byte character and string conversions, use the routines shown in Table 4-11.

Table 4-11. Multi-Byte Character and String Conversions

Routine	Description
`mblen`	If *s* is not a null pointer, the function examines the next *n* bytes. If the next *n* or fewer bytes form a valid multi-byte character, the number of bytes in the multi-byte character is returned. If they do not form a valid multi-byte character, `-1` is returned. If *s* points to the null character, `0` is returned.
`mbtowc`	Converts a multi-byte character pointed to by *s* to its wide character representation, storing the result in the array pointed to by *pwc*. The number of bytes in the original multi-byte character will be returned. At most, *n* bytes will be examined.
`wctomb`	Converts a wide character pointed to by *wchar* to its multi-byte representation, storing the result in the array pointed to by *s*. The number of bytes in the converted character is returned.
`mbstowcs`	Converts a sequence of multi-byte characters in the array pointed to by *s* into a sequence of corresponding wide character codes, storing the result in the array pointed to by *pwcs*, and stopping after *n* codes are examined or a null character is encountered.
`wcstombs`	Converts a sequence of wide character codes in the array pointed to by *pwcs* into a sequence of multi-byte characters codes and stores them in the array pointed to by *s*, stopping after *n* bytes are examined or a null character is encountered.

Wide Character Handling

Table 4-12 lists the WPI routines that are similar to the standard character and string processing routines described in Table 4-4. For more information on the WPI routines, see Appendix A or your `man` pages.

Table 4-12. Pre-WPI Routines vs. WPI Routines for Character and String Processing

Standard Routines	WPI Routines
char *strcat	wchar_t *wcscat
char *strncat	wchar_t *wcsncat
int strcmp	int wcscmp
int strncmp	int wcsncmp
char *strcpy	wchar *wcscpy
char *strncpy	wchar_t *wcsncpy
size_t strlen	size_t wcslen
char *strchr	char *wcschr
char *strrchr	wchar_t *wcsrchr
char *strpbrk	wchar *wcspbrk
size_t strspn	size_t wcsspn
size_t strcspn	size_t wcscspn
char *strstr	wchar_t *wcswcs
char *strtok	wchar_t *wcstok
int strcoll	int wcscoll
size_t strxfrm	size_t wcsxfrm

In addition, the following routines have been added:

Table 4-13. Additional Wide Character Handling Routines

Routine	Description
`int wcwidth`	Returns the number of column positions required for a wide character.
`int wcswidth`	Returns the number of column positions required for *n* wide characters.

Upshifting and Downshifting Wide Characters

WPI provides the following routines to upshift and downshift wide characters in a language-sensitive way. You can obtain more information about these routines by consulting your `man` pages.

Table 4-14. WPI Character and String Processing Routines

Routine	Description
`towupper(`*wc*`)`	If *wc* represents a valid lowercase wide character letter for the current language, `towupper(`*wc*`)` returns the integer character code of the upshifted value of *wc*; otherwise `towupper(`*wc*`)` returns *wc* unaltered.
`towlower(`*wc*`)`	If *wc* represents a valid uppercase wide character letter for the current language, `towlower(`*wc*`)` returns the integer character code of the downshifted value of *wc*; otherwise, `towlower(`*wc*`)` returns *wc* unaltered.

Identifying Wide Character Types

WPI provides tools to classify wide characters according to the rules of a language. Although non-internationalized ASCII versions of these routines have been a part of the standard C language for years, the enhanced internationalized versions can correctly identify a character type in any supported language. This assumes that a program has been initialized for local language information with `setlocale` and that a locale has been set up accordingly with the character classified as stated.

All the routines included in Table 4-15 below return a non-zero integer if the indicated condition is true; otherwise, they return `0`. For more information about these routines, see your `man` pages.

Table 4-15. WPI Character Identification Routines

Routine	Condition
`iswalpha(`*wc*`)`	Is *wc* a wide alphabetic character?
`iswupper(`*wc*`)`	Is *wc* a wide uppercase alphabetic character?
`iswlower(`*wc*`)`	Is *wc* a wide lowercase alphabetic character?
`iswdigit(`*wc*`)`	Is *wc* a wide decimal digit?
`iswxdigit(`*wc*`)`	Is *wc* a wide hexadecimal digit?
`iswalnum(`*wc*`)`	Is *wc* a wide alphanumeric character?
`iswspace(`*wc*`)`	Is *wc* a tab, new-line, space, or any wide character that creates "white space" in displayed text?
`iswpunct(`*wc*`)`	Is *wc* a wide punctuation character?
`iswprint(`*wc*`)`	Is *wc* a wide printing character?
`iswgraph(`*wc*`)`	Is *wc* a wide character with a visible representation?
`iswcntrl(`*wc*`)`	Is *wc* a wide control character?
`iswctype(`*wc*`)`	Is *wc* a wide character of any specified class type supported within the locale?

The function `wctype()` returns a value of type `wctype_t` that can be used in a subsequent call to `iswctype()`.

Numeric Formatting of Wide Characters

The numeric formatting routines in Table 4-16 have been internationalized and provide locale-sensitive results for wide character data.

Table 4-16. Wide Character Numeric Formatting Routines

Routine	Description
`wcstod`	Converts a wide character string to a `double`, correctly interpreting the radix character according to the currently active value of the `LC_NUMERIC` category.
`wcstol`	Converts a wide character string to a `long`.
`wcstoul`	Converts a wide character string to an `unsigned long`.

Wide Character Formatting of Date and Time

The parallel wide-character formatting function for `strftime` is `wcsftime`.

Table 4-17. Wide Character Date and Time Routines

Routine	Description
`wcsftime`	Similiar to `ctime` but accepts an optional format string which should be placed in a message catalog.

Wide Character Input and Output

WPI include character input and output routines. These routines are for use with wide characters only.

Table 4-18 lists the C programming language routines for character input and output and the equivalent wide character routines. For more complete information, see your `man` pages.

Table 4-18.
C Programming Routines vs. WPI Routines for Character Input and Output

C Routines	WPI Routines
`int getc`	`wint_t getwc`
`int getchar`	`wint_t getwchar`
`int fgetc`	`wint_t fgetwc`
`char *gets`	No equivalent.
`char *fgets`	`wchar_t *fgetws`
`int putc`	`wint_t putwc`
`int putchar`	`wint_t putwchar`
`int fputc`	`wint_t fputwc`
`int puts`	No equivalent.
`int fputs`	`int fputws`
`int ungetc`	`wint_t ungetwc`

Wide Character Formatting of Input and Output

The wide character conversion characters, `C` and `S`, can be used with `printf` and the other printing routines described under "Printing Formatted Output" earlier in the chapter as shown below:

Conversion Character	Conversion Function
`C`	format a single wide character
`S`	format a wide character string

The `C` and `S` wide character conversion characters can be also be used with `scanf` and the other scanning routines described under "Reading Formatted Input" earlier.

Examples Comparing Single-Byte Interfaces and WPI

The following examples illustrate how multi-byte programs may be fashioned from ones originally coded for single-byte codesets:

Example 1: Character Handling to Convert to Uppercase

Single-Byte Interfaces:

```
while (*p) {
   *q++ = toupper (*p++);
}
```

WPI:

```
mbstowcs (wp,p,n);  /* convert to wide character */
while (*wp) {
   *wq++ = towupper (*wp++);
}
```

Example 2: Character Input and Output

Single-Byte Interfaces:

```
while ((c = getc(f)) ! = EOF) {
   process_char(c); /*user-defined interface */
}
```

WPI:

```
while ((wc = getwc(f)) ! = WEOF) {
                     /* read the next character (not byte)
                        from the stream and stop if
                        an error is detected */
   if (ferror(f)
      process_wide_error(wc); /*user-defined interface */
   else
      process_wide_char(wc);  /*user-defined interface */
}
```

Example 3: Display Formatting

Single-Byte Interfaces:

```
while (c = *p++)  {          /* need at least 1 display
                                column  */
   if (column < 1) {         /* if no room left to display
                                1 more character, then
                                start a new line  */
      putchar('\n');
      column = MAX_COL;
   }
   putchar(c);
   column--;
}
```

WPI:

```
mbstowcs(wp,p,n);            /* convert to wide character */
while (wc = *wp++) {
   colwidth = wcwidth(wc); /* get the display width of the
                               character */
   if (column < colwidth) {
                            /* if there isn't enough room
                               to display the character,
                               start a new line */
      putwchar(L'\n');
      column = MAX_COL;
   }
   if (colwidth == -1)      /* if an error has occurred,
                               wc is unprintable */
       process_wide_error(wc);
   else {
       putwchar(wc);
       column -= colwidth;
   }
}
```

Example 4: Complete Programs Comparing Single-Byte and Wide Characters

For this example, a program is offered in two versions: the first works only for single-byte codesets, while the second is codeset independent.

Each program folds characters strings. A field size is specified defining the `WIDTH` for text displayed on the screen. As a given string is printed, any character whose display would fall outside the designated text region is "folded" onto the next line. For instance, if the `WIDTH = 5` and the string is `0123456789`, the result is:

```
01234
56789
```

Traditional Single-Byte Program Example

The following program works only for single-byte characters because multi-byte characters can potentially be split between bytes and treated as single-byte codes.

```
#include <stdio.h>
#include <locale.h>

#define WIDTH 5

main(argc, argv)
int  argc;
char **argv;
{
   unsigned char output_array[WIDTH], *output_ptr, *input_ptr;
   int c, counter;

   /* try to set the locale, even through it does not affect the program
      because there are no calls to routines that are affected by the locale */
   if (! setlocale(LC_ALL,"")) {
      fprintf(stderr,"error: cannot set locale\n");
   }
   input_ptr = argv[1];            /* initialize the pointers and counter */
   counter = 0;
   output_ptr = output_array;

   while (c = *input_ptr++) {      /* get a char until end of string */
     if (counter >= WIDTH {        /* if output array is complete, process it */

       *output_ptr = '\0';         /* null terminate the output array */
       puts(output_array);         /* print the output array */
       counter = 0;                /* reset counter */
       output_ptr = output_array; /* reset output pointer to beginning
                                      of array */
     }
     counter++;                    /* if output array not complete
                                      increment counter */
     *output_ptr++ = c;            /* set area pointed to by output_ptr
                 to c, then increment output_ptr */
   }
   *output_ptr = '\0';             /* null terminate the output array */
   puts(output_array);             /* print the output array */
}
```

Wide Character Program Example

The following code shows how the above program might be modified to operate correctly on single-byte *and* multi-byte data. It now uses wide characters and works for both HP-15 and EUC encoding schemes which were described in Chapter 2.

```
#include <stdio.h>
#include <stdlib.h>
#include <locale.h>
#include <nl_types.h>
#include <limits.h>
#include <wchar.h>

#define WIDTH 5                              /* max output line width */
#define MAX_INPUT_CHARS 100                  /* max chars in input */
#define MAX_MULTI (WIDTH*MB_LEN_MAX + 1)     /* max number of bytes in
                                                multi-byte output array */
#define MAX_WCHAR (WIDTH + 1)                /* max number of w_chars in
                                                w_char output array */
                                             /* NOTE: Assumes no printing
                                                char has zero width */

main(argc, argv)
int argc;
char **argv;
{
   wchar_t wc_in_array[MAX_INPUT_CHARS + 1]; /* input wchar string */
   unsigned char mb_out_array[MAX_MULTI];    /* output multi-byte string */
   wchar_t wc_out_array[MAX_WCHAR];          /* output wchar string */
   wchar_t *in_wc_ptr, *out_wc_ptr, wc;
   int counter, screen_size;
   nl_catd catd;

   if ( !setlocale(LC_ALL, "") ) {
       fputs("setlocale failed, continuing with \"C\" locale.", stderr);
       putenv("LC_ALL=");
       catd = (nl_catd)-1;
       }
   else
       catd = catopen("%%name%%", NL_CAT_LOCALE);

   counter = 0;                              /* initialize counter */
   in_wc_ptr = wc_in_array;                  /* set pointer to beginning of
                                                input wc array */
   out_wc_ptr = wc_out_array;                /* set pointer to beginning of
                                                output wc array */
   mbstowcs(wc_in_array, argv[1], MAX_INPUT_CHARS);
                                             /* convert input multi_byte
                                                string to wc array */
   while (wc = *in_wc_ptr++) {               /* get a character from the wc
                                                array until NULL */
      screen_size = wcwidth(wc);             /* get screen size of wc */
      if (counter + screen_size > WIDTH) {   /* if output array is complete
                                                process it */
         *out_wc_ptr = (wchar_t)0;           /* null terminate the output
                                                array*/
```

```
        wcstombs(mb_out_array, wc_out_array, MAX_MULTI);
                                              /* convert the wc array to a
                                                 multi-byte array */
        puts(mb_out_array);                   /* output the multi-byte array */
        counter = 0;                          /* reset counter to 0 */
        out_wc_ptr = wc_out_array;            /* reset wc output pointer to
                                                 beginning of wc array */
      }
      counter += screen_size;                 /* increment width counter */
      *out_wc_ptr++ = wc;                     /* add wc to the output array */
   }
   *out_wc_ptr = (wchar_t)0;                  /* terminate remaining output */
   wcstombs(mb_out_array, wc_out_array, MAX_MULTI);
                                              /* convert wc output array to
                                                 multi-byte */
   puts(mb_out_array);                        /* output the multi-byte array*/
}
```

Guidelines for Creating Internationalized Programs

- Whenever possible, evaluate the need to use WPI to handle character data unless you are *completely* sure your application will not support multi-byte codesets. (See "Guidelines for Using Wide Characters" earlier in the chapter.) WPI allows a compiled application to handle all system supported single- and multi-byte character encodings.
- Always *maintain data integrity*. Do not do *any* processing or examining of character data if you do not need to. If you are simply passing data through a routine or application, do not zero out the high bit of each byte, pad it into even-sized blocks, substitute linefeeds for carriage returns, etc.
- Never use the eighth bit of a character byte as a flag. This was a practice that grew out of the fact that ASCII is a 7-bit code. It is no longer acceptable.
- Never hardcode character constants. The run-time character set may be different from the compile-time character set. Comparing against a character constant may not work if the character has a different code in the run-time environment than it did in the compile-time environment. This is especially likely for characters not found in the ASCII set. If it is possible to put these values in files, where they can be changed, do so. If not, then at a minimum, assign symbolic names to them (like `slash`) so it will be easy to track down and change such codeset-dependent information later. Likewise, do not hardcode numeric constants to represent characters (like decimal 32 for "space").
- Never use ASCII rules for character transformation or identification. Upshifting characters by adding decimal 32 or testing for alphabetic characters by comparing against a numeric range, will probably not work for non-ASCII character sets. Use system supplied language/character-set sensitive routines for identifying or up/down shifting characters.
- When sorting data to be viewed by end-users, do not use numeric comparisons of strings or characters for collation. System routines exist for the appropriate language-sensitive collation of text strings. The only cases where comparisons based on a character's numeric representations should be used are when testing two strings for equality, or for hash tables, b-trees, etc. (structures which are never directly viewed or accessed by end-users). In

these cases, numeric comparisons provide higher performance and may be appropriate.

- Make sure you reserve enough space in arrays and other data structures to accommodate characters consisting of multiple bytes or wide characters. Since an international program supports character sets that contain multi-byte characters, the number of characters in a string is no longer equivalent to the number of bytes. You must allocate additional space to accommodate the larger character size.

- When processing multi-byte characters, it is no longer possible to simply scan a data stream looking for a byte whose bit pattern matches that of ASCII character. The byte that is matched may turn out to be merely one byte from a multi-byte character. Therefore, your program must search for *character matches*, not merely byte matches. You should use WPI to do this task.

- When reading characters, you must be careful to truncate excess input on character boundaries or else your data can be corrupted. For example, suppose that you allocate an 80-byte buffer for reading data. If the 80th byte read into the buffer is the first byte of a multi-byte character, then when the contents of another buffer are appended, the first byte of the appended buffer will be interpreted as the next byte of the multi-byte character. If you convert multi-byte data to wide characters for processing, then this will not affect you.

- Do not search for a single-byte character in multiple-byte data on a byte-by-byte basis. A given byte may represent either a single-byte character or part of a multiple-byte character. Use wide characters to search by character rather than by byte.

- Do not *back-scan*, truncate, or substitute multiple-byte data byte-by-byte. This is an extension of the rule above. Use wide characters to manipulate characters rather than individual bytes.

Using Message Catalogs for Your Applications

This section contains information on:

- placing messages in message catalogs
- searching for and locating message catalogs
- retrieving messages
- closing a message catalog
- issuing default messages
- creating the message text source file
- creating a new message catalog
- installing a message catalog

For information on localization of message catalogs, see Chapter 6.

Placing Messages in Message Catalogs

Program messages might include:

- information to the user, for example `file not found`
- responses from the user, for example `tomorrow` as used by the `at` command
- strings used to format other messages, for example `%1$d %2$s\n`

Without internationalization, these messages would ordinarily appear in the source program as quoted strings, such as:

```
printf("file not found\n");
    :
if ( strcmp(s, "tomorrow") == 0 ) ...
    :
```

To create a program that is internationalized for messages, you need to place messages into message catalogs.

The following summarizes the steps to use:

Step 1. Instead of coding messages into your source program, use message routine calls for the actual messages in your source program. The message routines will retrieve message text at run time.

Step 2. Create a message text source file. This file contains the text for messages that the above routines call. Because these message are in readable form, they are suitable for translation or other modification to meet the needs of international users.

Step 3. Generate the actual message catalog from the message text source file by using the text file as input to the `gencat` command. (More information on steps 2 and 3 will be discussed shortly.) The resulting file will contain the messages in binary form that are retrieved by the message routines.

Searching for and Locating Message Catalogs

Since neither message catalog file names nor locations are standard across implementations, you have considerable flexibility when naming your application's message catalogs and deciding upon their location in the file system.

The `NLSPATH` environment variable acts as the default path name or names used by the `catopen` command to locate the appropriate message catalog for opening. Its value is usually established by the system administrator.

`NLSPATH` allows for substitute field descriptors that permit the use of run-time information. Certain naming conventions are used by `NLSPATH`. Field descriptors consist of a `%` followed by a single character. The available field descriptors are summarized in Table 4-19.

Table 4-19. Summary of NLSPATH Field Descriptors

Field Descriptors	Substitution Values
`%L`	Current `LC_MESSAGES` or `LANG` setting.
`%N`	The *name* parameter passed to `catopen`.
`%l`	The language element of `LC_MESSAGES` or `LANG`.
`%t`	The territory element of `LC_MESSAGES` or `LANG`.
`%c`	The codeset element of `LC_MESSAGES` or `LANG`.

Note If the *oflag* argument of catopen is set to NL_CAT_LOCALE, the LC_MESSAGES *category* determines the message catalog to open. However, if you set *oflag* to 0, the LANG environment variable determines the message catalog to open. (See "Activating Program Messages" earlier in this chapter for more information.)

Refer to Chapter 6 if you are unfamiliar with the territory and codeset elements referred to in Table 4-19.

So, for example:

```
NLSPATH=/usr/local/lib/%L/%N.cat:./%N.cat
```

specifies two paths (separated by a ":") to search for a message catalog. The metacharacter, %, in the search path begins the substitute field descriptor, followed by the letters L and N. As shown in the table, %L is replaced by the currently set value for the LC_MESSAGES or LANG environment variable and %N is replaced by the value of the *name* argument passed to catopen.

Suppose that LC_MESSAGES=french and that catopen was called using the command catopen("prog", NL_CAT_LOCALE). To determine the value of NLSPATH, catopen will first attempt to open /usr/local/lib/french/prog.cat. If catopen is unable to open this message catalog, it will next attempt to open ./prog.cat. (If LC_MESSAGES or LANG is not set, a null string is inserted; thus, the first path would become /usr/local/lib/prog.cat with the probable result of a failure to find a catalog.)

If catopen doesn't find a message catalog with the path names specified in NLSPATH, it concludes the search with a default path. For example, on HP-UX the following default path is used:

```
/usr/lib/nls/%l/%t/%c/%N.cat
```

As shown in Table 4-19, %l is replaced by the *language* element of LC_MESSAGES or LANG, %t is replaced by the *territory* element of LC_MESSAGES or LANG, and %c is replaced by the *codeset* element of LC_MESSAGES or LANG.

When a ":" is used at the beginning of the NLSPATH description, it is equivalent to specifying %N. For example, given:

```
LC_MESSAGES=french
NLSPATH=:%N.cat:/nlslib/%L/%N.cat
```

`catopen` will attempt to open the following files in the indicated order:

1. `./name`
2. `./name.cat`
3. `/nlslib/french/name.cat`

Retrieving Messages

Once a message catalog has been opened using `catopen`, a program can retrieve messages from the catalog using the `catgets` routine. Parameters for `catgets` are as follows:

```
catgets(catd, set_num, msg_num, def_str);
    :
```

where:

catd	is the message catalog file descriptor returned by `catopen`.
set_num, *msg_num*	identifies the message to be retrieved (more details under "Creating the Message Text Source File" shortly).
def_str	is a default message string that is returned if the call fails. *def_str* ordinarily is the `C` locale message.

When retrieving messages, `catgets` uses an internal buffer which is overwritten on each call. This is rarely a problem since ordinarily a message is printed out immediately. (See "Multiple Messages in a `prinf` Call" in Chapter 5 for additional information.)

Closing a Message Catalog

Use `catclose` to close a message catalog file when a program no longer needs access to catalog. This can be done with the `catclose` call or simply let `exit` close the catalog file when the program terminates.

Issuing Default Messages

A program should make provision for instances in which an intended message catalog is not available. This might happen if the file system containing the catalog is not mounted or if there is no catalog for a desired language. Note that `catopen` does not take a default action if no catalog can be opened. Therefore, provisions for default messages must be made by the program. There are two general ways for handling this situation:

- The usual approach is to include a default message as the *def_str* in the `catgets` call, as described under "Retrieving Messages" above. If the `catopen` call fails, `(nl_catd)-1` is returned, indicating an invalid file descriptor. This causes `catgets` to fail with the result that *def_str*, the default message is returned. This is the recommended approach to handling default messages.
- Alternately, you can use a default message catalog. Note, however, that even the default message catalog may not be available (e.g., if the file system containing it were not mounted). Always consider the possibility of this occurrence if you are considering this approach. Programs that use this method should use error message numbers as the default string in your `catgets` calls.

If a message catalog is missing and you determine that the catalog is critical to the successful execution of the program, it would be best to issue a brief explanatory message to the user and terminate the program.

Creating the Message Text Source File

Prior to creating an actual message catalog, you first create a message text source file which contains the text of the messages you have isolated from the source program in a readable format. Each message is given a number which is used to identify the message when provided as the *msg_num* parameter in a `catgets` call.

For example, a simple message text file might be:

```
$ Comment:  Sample message text source file
1 text for message 1
2 text for message 2
```

Each message begins with a number, followed by a single space or tab, followed by text, and terminated by a new-line character. The message text is a valid C language string including spaces, tabs and \ (backslash) escapes, but without the surrounding quotes. Message numbers are unsigned integers and must be in ascending order but need not be consecutive. A line beginning with **$** followed by a single space or tab is treated as a comment. Note that comments in the message text source file will not be saved in the final message catalog.

For a large or related groups of messages, it may be useful to group the messages into sets. Message sets allow the programmer to cluster similar messages together within a catalog. For example, one set might contain just prompts while another set might contain error messages. A set is initiated by including a **$set** directive. Messages belong to the set specified by the most recently appearing **$set** directive. Like message numbers, set numbers are unsigned integers and must be in ascending order but need not be consecutive. The same message numbers can appear in different sets.

If a **$set** directive does not appear in the message text source file, messages are assigned to a default set `NL_SETD`. `NL_SETD` is defined in `<nl_types.h>`

A sample of a message text source file containing message sets might look like the following:

```
$set 100
$ user prompts
1 Text of message number 1
4 Text of message number 4
9 Text of message number 9
    :
$set 200
$ error messages
1 Text of message number 1
3 Text of message number 3
    :
```

To make leading or trailing blanks visible, use the **$quote** directive to specify a quote character. Then use the character both before and after the message to which space characters have been added. For example:

```
$ show blanks
$quote "
1 "   leading blanks"
2 "trailing blanks  "
```

For more details on the format of the message text source file, see your **man** page for **gencat**.

Creating a New Message Catalog

Once your message text source file is correct, you are now ready to complete the message catalog. To do so, use the **gencat** command to generate a message catalog from the message text source file.

For example, if **prog.msg** is your message text source file for **prog.c**, then by entering the following:

```
gencat prog.cat prog.msg
```

the message catalog, **prog.cat**, is generated for **prog.c**. As a result of using **gencat**, the message text source file is "compiled" into a binary message catalog which will be used to retrieve messages by **prog.c** at run time.

Figure 4-3 below summarizes this process.

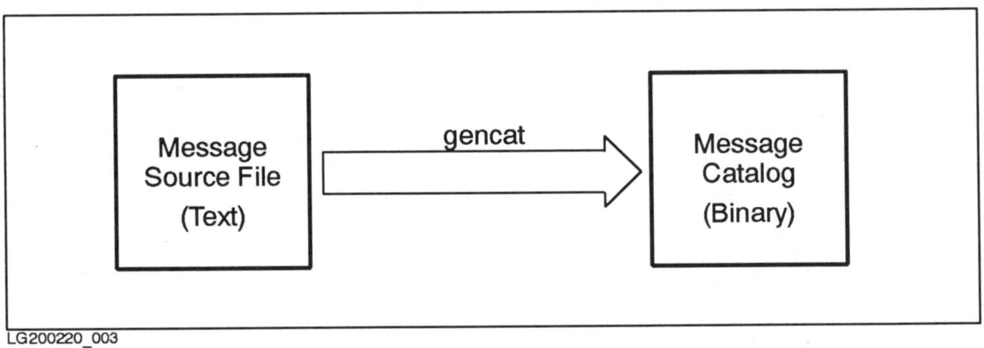

Figure 4-3. Using `gencat` to Generate Message Catalog

An Example of Programming with Message Catalogs

By way of summary, consider the following sample code. Suppose your program, `prog.c`, outputs the message `Hello friend` which may need to be localized in many languages.

When designed to make use of a message catalog, `prog.c` might look like this:

```
#include <stdio.h>
#include <nl_types.h>
#include <locale.h>
main()
{
nl_catd catd;
setlocale(LC_ALL,"");
catd = catopen("prog", NL_CAT_LOCALE);
printf(catgets(catd, NL_SETD, 1, "Hello friend\n"));
}
```

The message text source file might be:

```
$ message source file for prog.c
1 Hello friend\n
```

Compile the program as you ordinarily do. Thus:

```
cc -o prog prog.c
```

Additionally, you need to generate the actual message catalog:

```
gencat prog.cat prog.msg
```

Note that the default message string is included in the `catgets` call. This will be returned to the user if `catopen` fails. Since no `$set` directive is included in the message text source file, the default set, `NL_SETD`, is used in the `catgets` call within the source program.

Installing a Message Catalog

When you are satisfied that your program correctly accesses its message catalog, the catalog can be installed. Message catalogs for applications can be put in any location that can be referenced by the conventions of `catopen` and `NLSPATH`.

Guidelines for Using Messaging

Here are some overall guidelines which you should keep in mind when programming for messages.

- Provide a *cookbook* for the translator which contains the numbered messages and, carefully separated (e.g., by brackets), any additional explanatory information or paraphrasing they may need. A message that is obvious to you may not be at all clear to a translator. You should assume that the translator:
    - has a different native language than yours
    - is hundreds or thousands of kilometers away from you
    - is doing the translation months or years after you finish the program
    - is not familiar with C language programming
- All text that needs to be localized should be put in the message catalog. This includes such things as prompts, help text, error/warning/informational messages, format strings, and softkey definitions.
- Any text that will not be localized should not be put in the message catalog. For example, internal error messages for debugging purposes should not be included. Including unnecessary text will not affect program behavior but may prove to be confusing to a translator.
- Provide a unique, unambiguous message for each situation. A single message in your own language may appear to cover several different situations. However, when the message is translated into another language, each different situation may require a different local language translation.
- Do not split messages into separate messages in a message catalog unless absolutely necessary. The messages could be untranslatable if the word order changes when translated. If messages absolutely must be split, do so in a logical way. A large block of text, for example, should be split along sentence boundaries. (See "Splitting Up a Long Message" in Chapter 5 for related information.)
- Allow at least 60 percent extra space in text buffers and screen layouts to allow for text expansion when messages are translated. It may take more space to convey information in another language. Define these buffers in a localization cookbook or put them in comments at the beginning of each message catalog.

- Decide what to do if a message catalog cannot be found by your program. If the local language is vital to the operation of the program, you may want the program to issue a default error message and exit. If the local language is not vital to this part of your program, you might allow the program to continue to operate with a default locale (such as the `C` locale).
- Provide comments in the message catalog. Explain all C programming language parameters indicated by `%`.
- Avoid language that will be difficult to translate, such as culture-specific references, slang, and humor.

5

Special Programming Topics

This chapter provides additional coverage on programming issues. The topics covered include:

- initialization issues
- special considerations for messaging
- codeset conversion
- processing right-to-left languages

Initialization Issues

The following sections provide more detailed information on the `setlocale` and `catopen` routines.

Setting Multiple Locales

Recall from Chapter 4 that two parameters are necessary when calling the `setlocale` routine:

```
setlocale(category, locale)
```

`setlocale` can be used to set different *category* parameters to reflect multiple locales. For example, to initialize a program to run with French date and time conventions but with Spanish sorting conventions, the following `setlocale` calls could be used:

```
#include <locale.h>
     :
setlocale(LC_TIME,"french");
setlocale(LC_COLLATE,"spanish");
```

Such use, however, unnecessarily restricts the end user by defeating the goal of allowing the user to choose a local environment. Therefore, such an initialization is generally not recommended. A preferred way to get the desired effect would be to use the "Recommended Initialization" presented in Chapter 4 and to allow the user to set the internationalization environment variables when the program is run:

```
LC_TIME=french ; export LC_TIME
LC_COLLATE=spanish ; export LC_COLLATE
```

Setting the Message Catalog Path

The initial argument passed to the **catopen** routine can specify a complete path name for the message catalog being initialized, as in:

```
catd = catopen("/usr/special.cat", NL_CAT_LOCALE);
```

As is the case with initializing the local environment (above), such use defeats the flexibility of **catopen** and is therefore not recommended. A preferred way to get the desired effect would be to use the "Recommended Initialization" presented in Chapter 4:

```
catd = catopen("special", NL_CAT_LOCALE);
```

Then, allow the user to set the **NLSPATH** environment variable when the program is run:

```
NLSPATH="/usr/%N.cat" ; export NLSPATH
```

If an application must explicitly indicate the location of its message catalogs, the best approach is to modify **NLSPATH** from within the application by adding the appropriate path and then calling **catopen**. This will still allow the user to override the application and move the catalogs, if desired.

Programs That Call `exec`

For programs that call **exec**, it is recommended that the first program call **setlocale**. If the call is unsuccessful, use **putenv** to reset all the internationalization environment variables to ensure that the other programs don't repeat the unsuccessful **setlocale** call and issue additional error messages. For further information on **exec**, see the **man** page.

Special Considerations for Messaging

There are situations when you must be aware of additional considerations in programming for messaging.

Messages in Variables

Messages in variables require special treatment. Suppose, for example, you have the following code:

```
char *msg = "message";
     :
printf(msg);
     :
```

After converting the message, following the instructions in Chapter 4, the code would be:

```
char *msg = catgets(catd, set_num, msg_num, "message");
     :
printf(msg);
     :
```

However, this would generate a compile error. In order to prevent this, use the following conversion instead:

```
char *msg = "message";
     :
printf(catgets(catd, set_num, msg_num, msg));
     :
```

Messages in Arrays

Messages in arrays require somewhat more elaborate treatment. As an example, suppose your original source contains the following:

```
static char *msg_tbl[] = {
    "message 1",
    "message 2",
       :
    "message N"
    };
    :
printf(msg_tbl[i]);
    :
```

The correct conversion for this code would need to be:

```
printf(catgets(catd, set_num, msg_num, msg_tbl[i]));
    :
```

Note that *set_num*, *msg_num*, and message index `i` must be synchronized. `msg_tbl[0]` represents `message 1` and therefore 0 may not be used as a valid message number.

Multiple Messages in a `printf` Call

Suppose you have the following code:

```
printf("message 1", "message 2");
    ...
```

Because `catgets` overwrites its message string on each call, you should not convert this code as shown below:

```
printf(catgets(catd, set_num_1, msg_num_1, "message 1"));
printf(catgets(catd, set_num_2, msg_num_2, "message 2"));

    :
```

For this situation, it is necessary to copy one of the messages as shown:

```
char *m1[N];
    :
strcpy(m1, catgets(catd, set_num_1, msg_num_1, "message 1"));
printf(m1, catgets(catd, set_num_2, msg_num_2, "message 2"));
    :
```

Splitting Up a Long Message

Both `catgets` and `gencat` have limits on the length of messages they can handle. These limits may make it necessary to compose a large message, such as a help screen, from several smaller messages. Splitting a message must be done with care as a sentence fragment can create serious difficulties for the translation process. Whenever a message is split, each part should still express a complete sentence or idea. For further information, see the `-l` option under `man gencat`.

Checking for the Correct Message Catalog on HP-UX

The message system does not check to see that the correct catalog is used with a program. If an incorrect version of a message catalog is inadvertently installed, your program will issue messages but they will most likely not be correct. You may wish to add validation messages that contain the program revision code and the program locale so that the program can validate the message catalog it uses. This might be done as follows:

```
     :

char *p_rev =               /* program revision */
     "$Revision: 1.4 $";    /* catgets 1 */
char *c_rev;                /* catalog revision */
char *p_loc =               /* program locale */
     "C";                   /* catgets 2 */
char *c_loc;                /* catalog locale */

     :

c_rev = catgets(catd, NL_SETN, 1, p_rev);
if ( strcmp(c_rev, p_rev) != 0 ) {
    printf("program/message catalog revision mismatch\n");
    catd = (nl_catd)-1;
    }
p_loc = getenv("LC_MESSAGES");
c_loc = catgets(catd, NL_SETN, 2, p_loc);
if ( strcmp(c_loc, p_loc) != 0 ) {
    printf("program/message catalog locale mismatch\n");
    catd = (nl_catd)-1;
    }

     :
```

The example uses a *rcs*(1) `$Revision$` line (for more information, see `man co`). This allows the revision code to be updated automatically. The special comments `/* catgets 1 */` and `/* catgets 2 */` enable `findmsg` to find the validation messages. (See the discussion in the "Source Code Management on HP-UX" section in this chapter for related information.)

The message text source file for this program might contain:

```
$ Do not localize the revision line.
1 $Revision: 1.4 $
$ Do not localize the following line showing the locale.
2 C
```

Note the use of comments since both of these messages are potential problems for someone attempting to localize the program. (See "Guidelines for Using

Messaging" in Chapter 4 for a description of a "cookbook" to help the translator avoid errors.)

Libraries Using Message Catalogs

Library routines, as well as programs, can use message catalogs. For example, the C library routine `perror()` uses a message catalog and the routine can be used by a program that also uses its own message catalog.

All the considerations previously discussed for programs also apply to libraries. There are also some additional considerations.

In general, the scope of variables in a library routine is restricted to within the routine so that they will not conflict with the variables of the main program. The catalog descriptor must be declared so that there will be no conflict with the main program, since the main program may also use a message catalog.

Since a library routine might be called several times by a program, some consideration should be given to the way the message catalog file is opened. There are two general strategies:

- The easier strategy is to open the catalog when it is needed and close it when done. The file descriptor is used only when it is needed.
- For cases in which the library routine is called frequently, it may be desirable to avoid multiple opens and closes of the catalog. This can be coded as follows:

```
static nl_catd catd;
static int open_flag = FALSE;
      :
if ( ! open_flag ) {
      open_flag = TRUE;
      catd = catopen(...);
      }
      :
catgets(catd, set_num, msg_num, def_str);
      :
```

Once opened, the file descriptor remains in use for the remainder of the program. The catalog will be closed by `exit` at program termination. Note that this method cannot be used if `LC_MESSAGES` can change between calls to the routine.

Converting an Existing Program to Use Messaging on HP-UX

Information presented in Chapter 4 focused on creating a *new* program with messaging capability. But what if your program was previously written without message catalogs? Is there a straightforward way to convert it?

Fortunately, the conversion of an existing program to use messages can be automated to a substantial degree. As a result, even when writing a new program you may find it easier to write the program without messaging capability and, once the program is working, convert it to use messages.

The steps to use in the conversion process are listed below followed by more detailed information:

Step 1. Use the **`findstr`** command to find all the quoted strings in the source program and output them to a file.

Step 2. Review the list of quoted strings and remove any that are not messages.

Step 3. Use the **`insertmsg`** command to create the message text source file and to replace the string in the source program with a call to **`catgets`**.

Step 4. If necessary, edit the message text source file and/or the source program.

Step 5. Use the **`gencat`** command to create the message catalog from the message text source file.

Finding Strings in a Program

Use the **`findstr`** routine to extract source code strings and write them to an external file. Figure 5-1 shows an example.

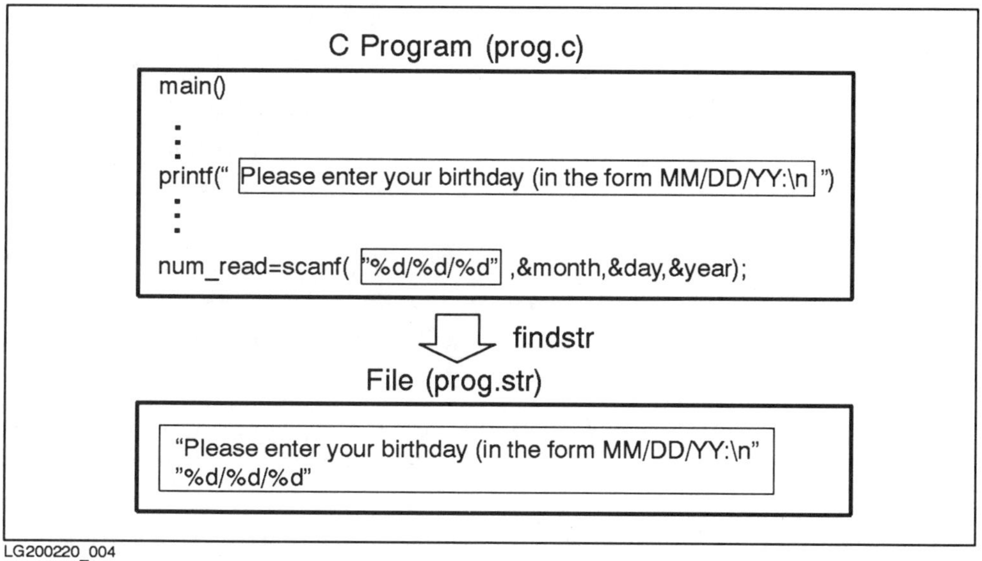

Figure 5-1. Using `findstr` to Locate String Constants on HP-UX

The command **`findstr`** examines a C source program and locates all string constants except for those that appear in comments. These strings, along with their surrounding quotes, are written to standard output or to a file, along with information indicating the position of the string in the source file. Thus, the command:

```
findstr prog.c > prog.str
```

creates the file, `prog.str`, containing a copy of each string found in `prog.c`.

Note that the **`findstr`** command expects the strings of your program to be syntactically correct with the quotes properly matched. To ensure that this is the case, it is good practice to use **`findstr`** only on tested programs.

Removing Non-Messages from the String File

Most of the strings in the string file are true messages for which localization is desirable. Some of the strings, however, may not be messages at all. For example, the type specifier for **`fopen`** is a string such as `"r"` or `"w+"`. Further, some format strings may not be localized. Therefore, the string file needs to be reviewed and any entries in the above categories should be removed.

When editing the string file, be careful not to modify the location information for those strings that are left in the file. Also, note that if the source file is changed, the string file may become invalid and need to be regenerated.

Using the `insertmsg` Command

Once you are ready to create a messaging version of your program, the **insertmsg** command helps to automate the process. **insertmsg** both creates the message text source file and replaces each string in the source program with a message routine call. That is, the **insertmsg** command:

- assigns a message number to each string in the string file and writes the numbered messages in a format suitable for use by **gencat**. This becomes the message text source file for the program.
- creates a copy of the source program in which each string identified in the string file is replaced by a **catgets** call with the assigned message number. The name of the new source program file becomes the name of the original source file with the prefix **nl_**.

For example, the command:

```
insertmsg prog.str > prog.msg
```

creates a message text source file **prog.msg** as well as a new source file. (If the **prog.str** file was created from **prog.c**, the new source file would be **nl_prog.c**.)

The processes involved are depicted in Figure 5-2.

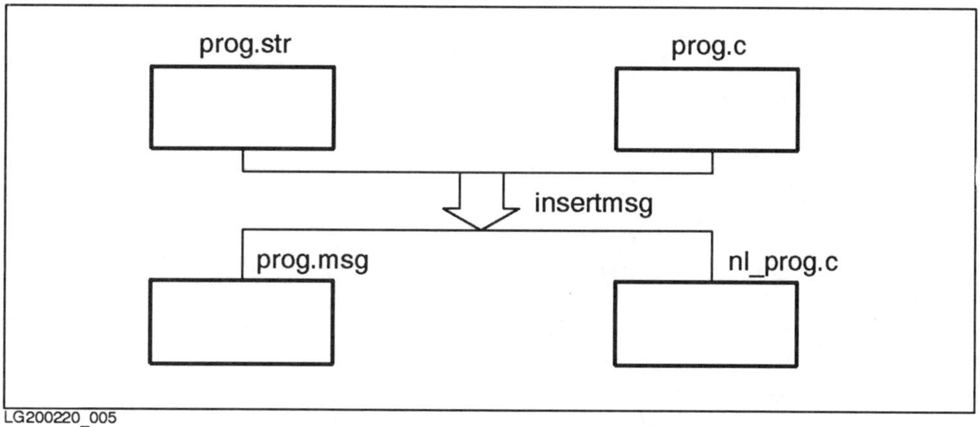

Figure 5-2. Using the `insertmsg` Command on HP-UX

Note The **`findstr`** and the **`insertmsg`** commands will not recognize the problem cases identified under the first three headers of this "Special Considerations for Messaging" section, converting them without comment. Some of these conversions will result in syntax errors from the compiler; others will give incorrect results with no prior warning. The recommended strategy is to let the compiler find syntax errors and to review the remaining conversions yourself for potential errors.

Editing the Source Program and/or the Message Text File

Your new source program may need some minor editing before it can be used. For example, a string such as:

```
... "string" ...
```

in the original source file will have been changed to:

... `catgets(catd, NL_SETN,` *msg_num*, `"string")` ...

The *msg_num* was assigned by **insertmsg**. You may need to provide definitions for **catd** and **NL_SETN**. This can be done by adding the following lines near the beginning of the program:

```
#include <nl_types.h>
#define NL_SETN 1
  .
  .
  .
nl_catd catd;
  .
  .
  .
catd = catopen("name", NL_CAT_LOCALE);
  .
  .
  .
```

Note Some of this code may ordinarily be part of your standard initialization. (See the section "Recommended Initialization" in Chapter 4 for additional information.) Also see the **-h** option under **man insertmsg** for information on code that can be generated automatically.

After these modifications, the new source program can be compiled and linked.

In many cases, the message text source file, **prog.msg** in the above example, will need no modification. However, if you are using sets, appropriate **$set** directives must be inserted.

Creating a Message Catalog

After any changes to the message text source file, the message catalog must be created using **gencat** as in the following example:

```
gencat prog.cat prog.msg
```

Figure 5-3 summarizes the steps to convert an existing program to use messaging:

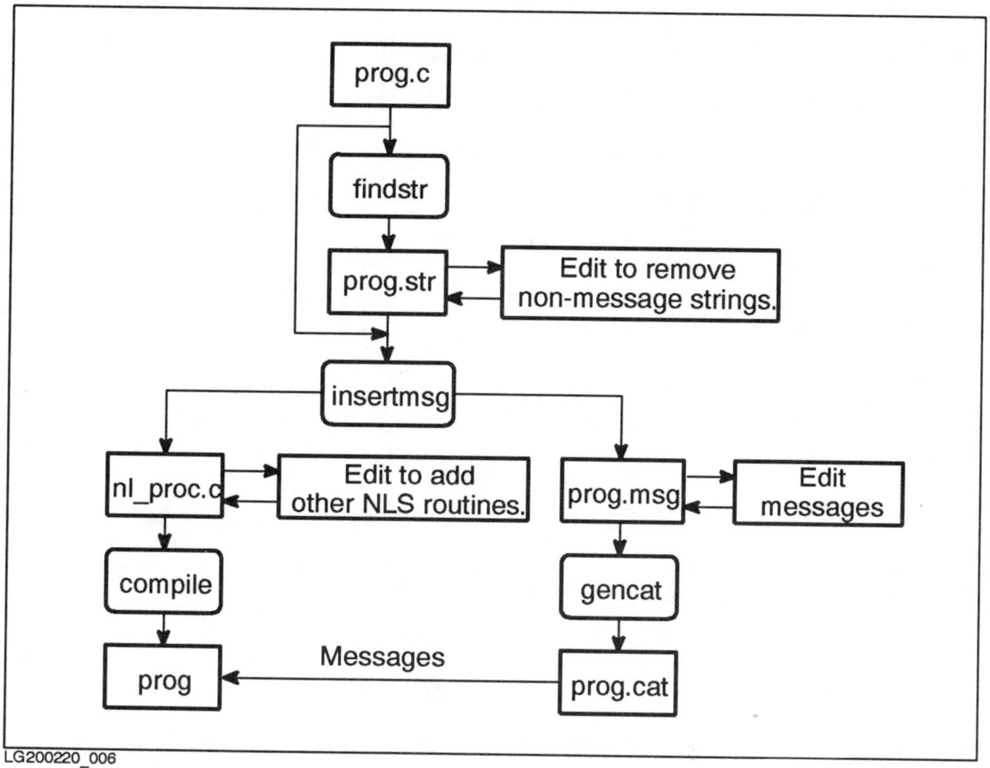

Figure 5-3. Converting a Program to Use Messaging on HP-UX

Testing a Message Catalog

Once you have an executable program and a message catalog, you can test the program to be sure that it correctly retrieves messages from the message catalog. If you use the "Recommended Initialization" presented in Chapter 4, the `NLSPATH` variable will make the testing easy.

For the following example, assume:

- The executable program is named `prog`.
- The catalog is opened by `catopen("prog",NL_CAT_LOCALE)`.
- The original text messages are in `prog.msg`.
- The `LC_MESSAGES` environment variable is unset.
- `setlocale` is called by `setlocale(LC_ALL,"")`.

Use the first four steps to prepare test directories and catalogs:

Step 1. Create a new directory.

```
mkdir ./test
```

Step 2. Make a copy of the message text source file.

```
cp prog.msg test.msg
```

Step 3. Modify the test messages to distinguish default messages from catalog messages. For example, you might add the word `(Test)` after every message.

```
vi test.msg
:
```

Step 4. Generate a message catalog with the modified messages.

```
gencat test/prog.cat test.msg
```

The catalog in directory `./test` is now ready for testing.

The next steps test the program for default messages and `test` messages:

Step 5. Set `NLSPATH`.

```
NLSPATH=./test/%L/%N.cat ; export NLSPATH
echo $NLSPATH
```

The path set within `NLSPATH` should be echoed.

Step 6. Test the catalog messages.

```
echo LC_MESSAGES = $LC_MESSAGES
prog
```

When the current setting for the `LC_MESSAGES` variable is NULL, the messages you see should be the modified test messages.

Step 7. Test the default messages.

```
LC_MESSAGES=C ; export LC_MESSAGES
echo LC_MESSAGES = $LC_MESSAGES
prog
```

When `LC_MESSAGES` is set to `C`, the unmodified messages should be displayed.

Using a Default Message Catalog

As described in Chapter 4, the usual approach to handling default messages is to use the `C` locale message as the default string in your **`catgets`** calls. This ensures that the program will be able to issue messages even if there is no message catalog available.

If your application must directly access a `C` locale message catalog for the default messages, the following code is suggested:

```
    ⋮
if (!setlocale(LC_ALL, "")) {
    fputs("Warning! call to setlocale failed\n", stderr);
    fputs("Continuing processing using the \"C\" locale\n", stderr);
    putenv("LC_ALL");
    catd = (nl_catd)-1;
    }
else
    catd = catopen("name", NL_CAT_LOCALE);
if (catd == (nl_catd)-1) {
    /* if necessary, user may save LC_MESSAGES at this point */
    putenv("LC_MESSAGES=C");
    setlocale(LC_MESSAGES,"");
    /* try NLSPATH */
    catd = catopen("name", NL_CAT_LOCALE);
    /* if necessary, user may restore LC_MESSAGES at this point */
    if (catd == (nl_catd)-1)
        /* try hard-coded path */
        catd = catopen("/usr/lib/nls/C/name.cat", NL_CAT_LOCALE);
    }
    ⋮
```

Source Code Management on HP-UX

The following present some suggestions and comments on the management of messaging source programs.

Keeping `nl_prog.c` Files

There are two approaches regarding the modified source files:

- You can rename the `nl_*` files to the original names and keep the modified version as the source program. This is the more commonly used approach. It eliminates the need for reconversion but means the source files have the `catgets` calls in them and are more awkward to read.
- Or, you can keep the original source files and convert them whenever they are modified. This eliminates the need to read the messaging statements

but means the source files must be converted whenever a change is needed. This approach may be feasible only if editing of the string file and converted source files is minimal or can be automated.

Multi-File Programs

If your program consists of a number of files, the conversion process is only slightly more complex than for a single file. The **findstr**, **insertmsg**, and **gencat** commands all take multiple file input and perform appropriately.

Adding a Message

Once your program provides message catalog support, you may need to add a message to the program. If you keep the original version of the source program (without the message catalog calls), adding a new message is done simply by adding the message to the source program and converting the program as above.

If you keep the **nl_*** version of the source program (with the message catalog calls), adding a message means that you must assign a message number to the new message and this new number must not conflict with those already used in the message catalog. To assign new message numbers, you will need a list of existing message numbers. These are available from two places: in the message catalog and in the source program.

The **dumpmsg** command will list the messages in a message catalog:

```
dumpmsg prog.cat > prog.msg
```

If there are multiple versions of the program, be sure that the message catalog and the source program are for the same version.

The **findmsg** command will list the messages in a source program:

```
findmsg prog.c > prog.msg
```

This method is generally preferred since it ensures that the message text source file agrees with the source program. However, note that you will lose all comments previously entered into the message catalog. The messages found are the quoted strings in **catgets** calls in the source program. If a program uses messages in variables, you must add special comments to the source program so that **findmsg** can find these messages. For example, a message in a variable and its corresponding **catgets** call would look like the following:

```
    :
char *msg = "message"; /* catgets msg_num */
    :
printf(catgets(catd, NL_SETN, msg_num, "message"));
    :
```

Both of the message listing commands produce, as output, a message text source file in a form suitable for input to **gencat**.

Once a message list is available, message numbers can be assigned to new messages and the source program appropriately modified with new **catgets** calls that have the newly assigned message numbers. The new messages can then be added to the message text source file and a new message catalog generated.

Although **gencat** can merge new messages into an existing message catalog, it is just as easy and less error prone to re-create the complete message catalog. Once the new **catgets** calls have been added to the source program, this can be done as follows:

Step 1. Remove previous message catalog to preclude update.

```
rm -f prog.cat
```

Step 2. Generate a message text source file with the new messages.

```
findmsg prog.c > prog.msg
```

Step 3. Generate the new catalog.

```
gencat prog.cat prog.msg
```

Step 4. List the new messages for review.

```
dumpmsg prog.cat | more
```

Using make Files

With the **.msg** and **.cat** file suffix conventions, it is possible to use **make** to automate message catalog creation. The following **make** file illustrates the procedure:

```
        :
    SOURCE = prog.c sub.c ...
        :
    all:    prog prog.cat
        :
    prog.msg $(SOURCE)
            findmsg $(SOURCE) >$@
        :
    .msg.cat:
            gencat $*.cat $*.msg
        :
```

The command:

```
make prog.msg
```

will generate the message text source file `prog.msg`. The command:

```
make prog.cat
```

will generate the message catalog `prog.cat` from the message text source file `prog.msg`.

Codeset Conversion

If you need to transport data between systems that use different codesets, you will probably need to convert codesets. To assist this conversion, several codeset conversion tools are available.

- The `iconv` *command* operates on files and converts characters from one codeset to another. Conversions can be performed within and between a number of standard codesets, including HP-specific codesets.
- When you convert codesets within an application, you can avoid the overhead involved in a command line call to a systems routine by using library routines instead.
- **Native Language Input/Output (NLIO)**, an HP-UX product, provides some other routines for Asian languages.

More information on the `iconv` command and the `iconv()` routines follows.

The Character Conversion Command

The syntax for evoking the **iconv** command is:

iconv -f *fromcode* -t *tocode* *[file...]*

where:

fromcode	Identifies the source codeset.
tocode	Identifies the target codeset.
[file...]	Identifies the input file or files, if any. If no arguments are specified, standard input is read. Results are written to standard output.

For example, to convert the contents of file, **hp**, from the HP-specific codeset ROMAN8 to ISO 8859-1 and redirect the results into the file **standard**, use:

```
iconv -f roman8 -t iso8859_1 hp > standard
```

For more information, see **man iconv**.

Standard Conversion Routines

There are three standard conversion routines: `iconv_open`, `iconv()`, and `iconv_close`.

The `iconv_open` routine is used prior to the `iconv()` call. It performs necessary initializations for codeset conversions.

The syntax of `iconv_open` is as follows:

iconv_t iconv_open (const char **tocode*, const char **fromcode*);

where:

tocode	Identifies the target codeset.
fromcode	Identifies the source codeset.
`iconv_t`	Acts as a conversion descriptor and function return value.

The `iconv()` routine allows code conversion at the application level.

The syntax of iconv() is as follows:

```
#include <iconv.h>

size_t iconv(iconv_t cd, const char **inbuf, size_t *inbytesleft,
             char **outbuf, size_t *outbytesleft);
```

where:

cd	is the conversion descriptor returned from the prior call to iconv_open.
inbuf	is an array containing the characters in the original codeset.
outbuf	is an array containing the characters in the converted codeset.
inbytesleft	provides the number of bytes in the input buffer.
outbytesleft	provides the number of bytes in the output buffer.
The type size_t	is defined in the header <stddef.h>

The iconv_close routine is used subsequent to the iconv() call. It closes the conversion descriptor cd and any other resources opened by iconv_open. Zero is returned if the routine is successful; otherwise -1 is returned. The syntax of this routine is:

```
void iconv_close(inconv_t cd);
```

An HP-Specific Conversion Routine

There is an HP-UX conversion routine, iconvlock, that can be used to initialize lock-shift information. The syntax of this routine is:

```
int iconvlock(iconv_t cd, int direction, int lock, const char *s);
```

For more information on the HP-specific iconvlock routine, see *iconv*(3C) in the *HP-UX Reference* or type man 3C iconv on an HP-UX system.

Processing Right-to-Left Languages on HP-UX

Processing right-to-left languages requires the programmer to deal with issues of data directionality that are not ordinarily a concern.

Data directionality refers to two properties of text:

- the direction the language is naturally read. This can be referred to as the **mode** of the language.
- the order in which characters are written, stored in a file, or displayed. This is referred to as the **order** of the language.

The mode is usually either:

- left-to-right (Latin-based languages)
- right-to-left (non-Latin-based languages, such as Arabic and Hebrew)

The order is either:

- keyboard: the order in which the user enters keystrokes.
- screen: the order in which characters are displayed.

Some codesets contain Latin and non-Latin characters so that it is possible to mix left-to-right and right-to-left text. If we use `L`*i* to indicate a Latin character, `N`*i* to indicate a non-Latin character, and *i* to indicate the order in which the character is typed, the mixed text:

```
N1 N2 L3 L4 N5 N6 L7 L8
```

entered on a terminal configured for right-to-left display would appear as:

```
L7 L8 N6 N5 L3 L4 N2 N1
```

For additional information on directionality, see *hpnls*(5) in the *HP-UX Reference*.

Two commands are available to manage data directionality. The command `forder` allows users with screen data to use programs that do not support screen order data. It converts the order of characters in a file from screen order to keyboard order, or from keyboard to screen order. For example, `sort` cannot sort screen order data. However, such data could be sorted by:

```
forder file1 |          # put in keyboard order for sort
sort |                  # sort it
forder > file2          # put back in screen order
```

Data mode and order information is specified by the **LANGOPTS** environment variable. To set the **LANGOPTS** environment variable using the Bourne or Korn Shell, enter:

```
LANGOPTS=[mode][_order] ; export LANGOPTS
```

where:

mode may be either **l** (for Latin) or **n** (for non-Latin). Non-Latin mode is assumed for values other than **l** and **n**.

_order describes the data order of a file and may be either **k** (for keyboard) or **s** (for screen).

For further details on the **LANGOPTS** environment variable, see *environ*(5) in the *HP-UX Reference*.

Since most printers are designed for printing left-to-right languages, printing right-to-left data requires special formatting. The command **nljust** provides this special formatting. It aligns such data with the right margin and composes the data in right-to-left print order. For example, **nljust** would typically be used as a filter with the **lp** and **pr** commands, such as in:

```
pr file | nljust | lp
```

As with **forder**, **nljust** also gets mode and order information from the **LANGOPTS** variable.

For special situations that cannot be handled by data ordering commands, the routine **strord** converts between screen order and keyboard order and can be used to provide any special processing that may be needed.

As a simplified example, consider a program that reads data in either keyboard or screen order, and writes it to a terminal in screen order. The relevant portions of the program are:

```
    :
#include <nl_types.h>
    :
char *lopts;
    :
lopts = getenv("LANGOPTS");       /* "m_o" m = mode, o = order */
    :
fscanf(..., src, ...);            /* read in current mode/order */
if ( lopts[2] == 'k' )            /* if order is keyboard order */
    strord(dst, src, lopts[0]);   /* re-order before write */
fprintf(..., dst, ...);           /* write data */
    :
```

6

Localizing Internationalized Software

This chapter discusses information and tasks that are needed to use internationalization features at a particular geographic site.

The topics discussed include:

- tasks to be performed at the system level
- localizing message catalogs
- converting between codesets

HP-UX System-Level Tasks

System-level tasks may be performed by a variety of individuals depending upon the specific site. Such individuals might include system administrators, systems programmers, computer operators, and knowledgeable general users. Regardless of who performs them, these tasks are essential for the proper functioning of internationalized programs. This section covers the following tasks:

- understanding HP-UX NLS directory and file structure
- resetting the default NLS environment
- installing message catalogs
- installing files for new locales
- using the appropriate peripherals

Understanding the HP-UX NLS Directory and File Structure

Directory and file names for internationalization information vary from system to system. Table 6-1 shows HP-UX specific directories and file locations for NLS information that is used by HP-UX commands and libraries.

Table 6-1. HP-UX NLS Directories and Files

Directory/File Name	Type of NLS Information
`/usr/lib/nls`	This is the parent directory for NLS information.
`/usr/lib/nls/config`	This readable ASCII file identifies the names of all available locales, including any user-defined locales (see Chapter 7, "Creating a New Language Environment," for more information). It also contains corresponding locale-ID numbers.
`/usr/lib/nls/`*locale*	This directory is present for each installed locale.
`/usr/lib/nls/`*locale*/*locale.inf*	These files contain locale-specific data and are generated by **`localedef`**. (See Chapter 7 for more information on **`localedef`**.)
`/usr/lib/nls/`*locale*/*locale.ext*	These files, if present, contain locale-dependent processing information used by the WPI routines.
`/usr/lib/nls/`*locale*/**.cat*	These are localized message catalog files.

Note

Locale names are implementation specific.

For X/Open, locale names are of the form:

language[_territory][.codeset][@modifier]

where:

_territory is an optional variation of a language according to geographic considerations, such as for designating the French Canadian language.

.codeset is an optional variation of a language according to the codeset used. For example, `german.iso88591` represents the German language with a codeset of ISO 8859-1; `german` without *.codeset* by default has a codeset of ROMAN8.

@modifier is an optional variation of a language allowing for the selection of additional localization information, such as character ordering versus lexicographical ordering. (See "Collating Sequence" in Chapter 2 for more on these methods of ordering.)

At the present time, HP-specific locale entries in `/usr/lib/nls/config` conform to the *.codeset* standard but use a slightly different format for territory designation. For example, the name of the French Canadian ROMAN8 codeset is `c-french`. (Refer to Appendix C for a complete list of HP-UX language codesets.)

Upon installation, there will be a corresponding subdirectory created for each distinct HP locale name reflecting the unique *.codeset* extension or territory designation. For example, `/usr/lib/nls/config` contains the following entries:

```
    ⋮
french
french.iso88591
c-french
c-french.iso88591
    ⋮
japanese
japanese.euc
    ⋮
```

If each of these `config` entries are installed, then you will be able to find each of the following directories:

```
/usr/lib/nls/french
/usr/lib/nls/french/iso88591
/usr/lib/nls/c-french
/usr/lib/nls/c-french/iso88591
/usr/lib/nls/japanese
/usr/lib/nls/japanese/euc
```

Resetting the Default NLS Environment

The default NLS environment for the system is the `C` locale. However, other system default values can be set by the system administrator to reflect the needs of the local user community. To do this, include statements in `/etc/profile` and `/etc/csh.login` that set the NLS environment variables to the desired values.

Installing Message Catalogs

Once message catalogs have been translated into a local language (see "Localizing Message Catalogs" shortly), these localized messages should be installed in the appropriate location. Message catalogs for HP-UX commands and libraries should be installed in the `/usr/lib/nls/`*locale* directory. If your HP-UX system has locales with *_territory* or *.codeset* extensions, be sure to locate the correct directories as described above under "Understanding the HP-UX NLS Directory and File Structure."

Message catalogs for applications can be put in any location that can be referenced by the conventions of `catopen` and `NLSPATH`. (See *catopen*(3C) and *environ*(5) in the *HP-UX Reference* for more information.) The selection of a location and the naming of these local message catalogs can often be made by a local programmer in consultation with the system administrator. Such location and naming may necessitate a change to the system default value of NLSPATH. If it does, the system administrator should determine the new value and make the required change to the NLSPATH setting in /etc/profile and /etc/csh.login. The system administrator should then make sure all users are notified of this change.

Installing Files for New Locales

The procedure for installation of the necessary files for a new locale is identical to that for installing any additional software. Once a locale is installed, the information it contains can be used by any application program requesting it.

Normally, HP-UX is shipped with files for all supported locales.

Using the Appropriate Peripherals

Not all coded character sets are supported on all peripherals, so you need to be sure to use peripherals which support the desired character set. In a non-ASCII or multiple language environment, your peripherals will need to support the appropriate coded character sets. Hewlett-Packard provides printers, plotters, keyboards, and terminals which support HP single- and multi-byte coded character sets, such as the ISO 8859-1 coded character set for Western Europe. In some cases, you may need special software in order to operate these peripherals, such as NLIO software for Asian peripherals.

Localizing Message Catalogs

This section presents information about how to localize messages displayed by internationalized software. Localized messages enable presentation in the local language of the user.

For UNIX commands and applications that have message catalogs, you can create a local language interface by:

- finding the messages requiring translation
- producing a readable copy of the messages in their original language
- translating the messages into the desired language
- formatting messages
- creating and installing a message catalog containing the translated messages

Finding the Messages Requiring Translation

There are no standard locations for either UNIX command message catalogs or message catalogs for applications. Nor are there standard naming conventions for message catalog files.

C Locale Messages on HP-UX

To determine which HP-UX commands have message catalogs, enter:

```
ls /usr/lib/nls/C/*.cat
```

For each HP-UX command that has message catalogs, there will be a file `/usr/lib/nls/C/`*command*`.cat` listed.

Messages from Other Locales on HP-UX

HP-UX currently provides localized message catalogs in Japanese, Korean, Traditional Chinese, Simplified Chinese, German, and French. These catalogs for HP-UX commands, if installed on your system, will be located under the appropriate `/usr/lib/nls/`*locale* directory and also have a `.cat` suffix. After determining the desired locale, use `ls` to list out the message catalogs.

You will only need to translate HP-UX command messages if the desired language is not listed above.

If any of the above localized command message catalogs were not included with your system, or if you want to check if a particular application has localized message catalogs, you should contact the HP sales or marketing office in your area for a list of available localized products. HP provides localized messages in the above major languages at no additional cost.

Producing a Readable Version of Messages on HP-UX

Since an HP-UX message catalog file ending in `.cat` is not readable itself, you will need to create a readable version. This is done with the HP-UX **`dumpmsg`** command. For example, to get a message text source file of the `C` locale messages for **`date`**, enter:

```
dumpmsg /usr/lib/nls/C/date.cat > date.msg
```

The **`.msg`** file is a message text source file of the messages and is ready for translation to a native language.

Translating Messages

To translate messages, follow these steps:

Step 1. Set the `LC_MESSAGES` or `LANG` environment variable to the appropriate locale for the language you wish to translate into.

Step 2. Bring up the message text source file in your chosen editor. For example, enter:

```
vi date.msg
```

Step 3. You are now ready to begin to translate the messages to the target language.

Note

As described shortly under "Creating and Installing Localized Message Catalogs," the message text source file (in the previous example, the `.msg` file) must be in a format suitable for input to `gencat`, the UNIX command for creating a message catalog. You must preserve the format and you must leave the message numbers and the set numbers unchanged.

If the translated message is longer than 80 bytes per line, do not hit carriage return in order to start a new line. Instead, do one of the following:

- Continue typing to allow the word to "wrap-around" to the next line. (You need to be aware that your editor may have a physical line limit that will curb the length of the physical line.)
- Or, type a \ (backslash) before the carriage return and continue typing in the first column of the next line.

If you want to signify where a carriage return will appear in the message when it is output to the user, type `\n`. When output to the user, the text following the `\n` will begin on a new line.

The person or persons who created the original message catalog should have created a "cookbook" to help with translation problems. This should help with most problems you might encounter. If this is not available or complete, here are some possible translation problems you might encounter along with possible solutions:

- The meaning of a message or of a substitution parameter may be unclear or ambiguous so that the correct translation is not apparent.
- There may be unspecified size constraints on the message. For example, it may be displayed in a space with a fixed length.
- There may be parts of a message that should not be translated. For example, messages for a command may contain the command name.
- Some messages might be used together and need to be translated as a pair.

If you encounter translation problems, there are several possible solutions you might try:

- Experiment with the program to see if you can determine the intended behavior.
- Attempt to locate the developer of the program and ask for a clarification.
- Find and ask someone who has previously localized the program.

Formatting Messages

Messages that contain order-sensitive information, such as the date or currency information, will often need to be rearranged for display in different locales. For example, the date:

```
1/25/93
```

as displayed for an American locale may need to be displayed differently outside of the U.S.

This is accomplished by treating the format string as a message that can be modified within your local message catalog. Refer to "Formatting of Input and Output" in Chapter 4 for further details.

Creating and Installing Localized Message Catalogs

Once the message text source file has been translated to the target language, you must generate a message catalog containing the newly translated messages. For example, to create a message catalog from the translated `date.msg` message text source file you have edited as described above, use it as input to the `gencat` command:

```
gencat date.cat date.msg
```

The new message catalog, `date.cat` is now ready for installation in the appropriate directory. (See "Installing Message Catalogs" earlier in the chapter for HP-UX installation information.)

Note that a message catalog contains no information to indicate where it should be installed. To help ensure that the message catalog is installed in the proper directory, you might want to create a script file to deliver along with the catalog file that is able to install the catalog in the correct location.

Once the new message catalog is installed, be sure to verify the correct installation. (See "Testing Your Language Environment" in Chapter 3.)

Converting Between Codesets

In Chapter 5, the use of the `iconv` command and the `iconv` interfaces to convert data from one codeset to another was presented. You should note that these programming features cannot be used to convert between different *languages* (e.g., between French and Russian), just between different *codesets* (such as between ISO 8859-1 and ISO 8859-5, which represent the two standard codesets for French and Russian).

Refer to "Codeset Conversion" in Chapter 5 for more information.

7

Creating a New Language Environment

A UNIX system may or may not include files for multi-language environments. HP-UX, for example, is shipped with binary files for many locales. These locales cover most languages. (See Appendix C for a complete listing.) Other vendors may ship actual source code instead of binary files for each locale.

If none of the existing locales that come with your system are appropriate to your needs, you can create a locale that meets your specific requirements.

This is most easily done if an existing locale is similar to the one you want to create. If so, you can get a copy of the locale description, modify the description so that it conforms to your needs, then install it as a new locale. These steps are described below.

If there is no existing locale that is similar to what you need, see "Creating a New Locale Using a `localedef` Script" presented shortly.

Note The examples presented in this chapter assume that you are using an HP-UX system. They also assume you are examining the American locale called `american` on HP-UX. It may be unavailable or named differently on other systems.

Modifying an Existing Locale

Suppose you need a locale that is the same as the one that is installed as the American locale except that it has a different date format.

For the `american` locale, `date` will produce output of the form:

```
Fri, May 7, 1993 04:37:33 PM
```

Suppose the desired format is:

```
Fri, 7 May 1993, 04:37:33 PM
```

The format for `date` is controlled by the `d_t_fmt` and `d_fmt` keywords of the `LC_TIME` locale category, as will be elaborated on shortly. To change these values, follow these steps:

Step 1: Get a Copy of a Locale Description

To get a copy of the `american` locale on HP-UX, execute `localedef` with the `-d` option. This option is specific to HP-UX and creates an editable script of the existing locale:

```
localedef -d american > new_locale
```

The above command places a copy of the locale's script in `new_locale`.

Note If you are working on a system which comes with a source file for the American locale, you will not need to convert from a binary to an editable file.

Step 2: Modify the Locale Description

Next, you can modify the script to define the desired locale by editing the copy:

```
vi new_locale
```

The script for the `american` locale will contain the following entries:

```
    ⋮
langname        "american"
langid  1
    ⋮
LC_TIME
d_t_fmt "%a, %b %.1d, %Y %I:%M:%S %p"
d_fmt   "%a, %b %.1d, %Y"
t_fmt   "%I:%M:%S %p"
day_1   "Sunday"
    ⋮
END LC_TIME
    ⋮
```

To get the desired formatting, you will need to change the `d_t_fmt` and `d_fmt` lines in the script. See **`man strftime`** for the meaning of the various directives shown, that is, the characters preceded by `%` in the above example. (On HP-UX, you'll also need to substitute your chosen new locale name (*locale_name*) and locale identification number (*locale_id_no*) into the script as shown below. These values must not conflict with existing values, and the locale number must be in the range 901-999. (See "Using `localedef` Script Syntax" for more information.)

```
    ⋮
langname        "locale_name"
langid          locale_id_no
    ⋮
LC_TIME
d_t_fmt "%a, %.1d %b %Y %I:%M:%S %p"
d_fmt   "%a, %.1d %b %Y"
t_fmt   "%I:%M:%S %p"
    ⋮
END LC_TIME
    ⋮
```

Step 3: Install the New Locale Description After you have changed the locale description, install it in the system by executing:

```
localedef -i new_locale
```

Note

You will need superuser privileges to do this installation. If you do not have these privileges, ask your system administrator to install `new_locale`.

To verify correct installation of the new locale, run `locale -a` to see that the new locale is displayed.

On HP-UX, you can:

- Examine `/usr/lib/nls/config` to see that *locale_name* is listed with *locale_id_no*.
- Verify that a directory `/usr/lib/nls/`*locale_name* exists.
- Verify that a file `/usr/lib/nls/`*locale_name*`/locale.inf` exists.

Now set `LANG` or `LC_TIME` to the new locale name and verify that `date` formats the date as desired.

Creating a New Locale Using a `localedef` Script

The above example shows how to modify an existing locale script to create a language definition for a new locale. This section describes the structure and syntax of a script to be processed by **`localedef`** in detail, making explicit the "rules" you must adhere to when defining a new locale.

In general, the locale categories in Table 7-1 make up a language definition included in your script.

Table 7-1. Primary Categories of a Locale Script

Locale Categories	Function
LC_COLLATE	Affects the behavior of the regular expressions and the internationalized string collation functions.
LC_CTYPE	Affects the behavior of character classification and conversion functions.
LC_MESSAGES	Affects the language in which messages are to be displayed; also affects affirmative and negative response expressions.
LC_MONETARY	Affects the behavior of functions which handle monetary values.
LC_NUMERIC	Affects the handling of the radix character in the formatted input/output functions and the string conversion functions.
LC_TIME	Affects the behavior of the time conversion functions.
LC_ALL	Contains language-specific information which does not belong to any of the above categories.

In creating a new locale script, use the following general principles:

- All information in the script (except the language name, language id, revision number, comment character, and escape character) belongs to one of the above categories.
- A category definition begins with the name of the category. The end of each definition is identified by `END` followed by the name of the category.
- Category names can be listed in any order in a `localedef` script.
- All category specifications are optional. If a category is not specified, the `C` locale is set up as the default for that category.
- A single character may be represented in any of the following ways:
  - as a symbolic name enclosed within angle brackets (`<` and `>`). In such cases, a "charmap" must be available mapping the symbols with their character encodings. Many implementations use this representation.
  - as the character itself
  - as a hexadecimal value
  - as an octal value
  - as a decimal value
  - as a character within single quotes ('). This representation is specific to HP-UX and is the one used in the examples in this chapter.

  So, for example, you might use any of the following representations:

`<7> <7>; <7>`	*symbolic name*
`7 7; 7`	*character representation*
`\x37 \x37;\x37`	*hexadecimal representation*
`\d55 \d55;\d55`	*decimal representation*
`\067 \067;\067`	*octal representation*
`'7' '7'; '7'`	*HP-UX representation*

Using `localedef` Script Syntax

Table 7-1 shows the basic categories of a `localedef` script. In addition to the basic categories, the syntax of the `localedef` script provides for the specification of subcategories, called keywords, for each category. These are used by listing a predefined keyword followed by one or more expressions that specify applicable characteristics of the language. These keywords will be described in the subsequent sections.

`localedef` Script Header Keywords on HP-UX

HP-UX's `localedef` recognizes five keywords that do not belong to any of the basic categories, but rather, form a header for the locale definition script, uniquely identifying the language. These are shown in Table 7-2.

Table 7-2. `localedef` Header Keywords on HP-UX

Keyword	Function
`langname`	To define a string identifying the name of the language. This keyword is required by **`localedef`** if the command line invoking **`localedef`** does not contain the *locale_name*. (See *localedef*(1M) in the *HP-UX Reference*.)
`langid`	To define a decimal number identifying the language ID. This keyword is required by **`localedef`** if the command line invoking **`localedef`** does not contain the *locale_name* (see *localedef*(1M) in the *HP-UX Reference*). The language ID specified should be in the range 1 to 999. (A user-defined language should be restricted to a language ID in the range of 901 to 999.)
`revision`	To define a string identifying the revision number of the **`locale.inf`** file. (See Table 6-1.) The string must contain no more than 6 characters all of which are digits with one optional decimal point (.) character.
`comment_char`	To define a single character which will act as the start of a comment within the script. The default **`comment_char`** is **`#`**. All characters from **`comment_char`** to the end of the current line are ignored.
`escape_char`	To define a single character which will act as an escape character within the script. The default **`escape_char`** is \. The **`escape_char`** is used to escape **`localedef`** metacharacters, removing special meaning. It is also used in the character constant decimal, octal, and hexadecimal formats representing byte values.

The following example shows the header of a `localedef` script for the `american` locale:

```
langname      "american"
langid           1
revision      nnn.nn
comment_char  #
escape_char   \
```

localedef **Script** copy **Keyword**

localedef recognizes one keyword, copy, in all of the locale categories. This keyword is used to define a string naming another valid locale available on the system. This causes the category in the locale being created to be a copy of the same category in the named locale. Since the copy keyword defines the entire category, if used, it must be the only keyword in the category.

LC_ALL Keywords on HP-UX

The keywords shown in Table 7-3 are included as part of the LC_ALL category.

Table 7-3. LC_ALL Keywords on HP-UX

Keyword	Function
direction	To define a string indicating a text direction. If the null string or 0 is specified, text direction is left-to-right; if 1 is specified, text direction is right-to-left. In all cases, a top-to-bottom format is assumed.
context	To define a string indicating if character context analysis is required. If the null string or 0 is specified, no context analysis is required. If 1 is specified, Arabic context analysis is required.

Shown below is an example using the LC_ALL keywords from a localedef script. The script follows C programming language conventions; strings are enclosed in double quotes. Comment lines begin with #:

```
#####################################################

# LC_ALL category

LC_ALL
direction  "1"
context ""
END LC_ALL
```

In this example, the text direction will be from right-to-left and no context analysis will be required.

LC_COLLATE Keywords

The keywords shown in Table 7-4 are included as part of the LC_COLLATE category.

Table 7-4. LC_COLLATE Keywords

Keyword	Function
collating-element	To define a multi-character collating element composed of two characters.
collating-symbol	To allow for the definition of symbols between the **order_start** and **order_end** keywords.
order_start	To denote the start of the list of character entries that define the collating sequence.
order_end	To mark the end of the list of character entries that define the collating sequence.

Note **collating-symbol** is not currently available for users of HP-UX (as of the 9.0 version).

A collation sequence defines the relative ordering of characters by a computer in a particular locale. This order is expressed in terms of collation values that are assigned to each of the characters.

A character to be collated may be a single character or a multi-character collating element. The collating order is achieved by explicitly ordering the characters and collating elements between the **order_start** and **order_end** keywords. The collating order entry is of the form:

collating-identifier [*primary-weight*; [*secondary-weight*; *nth-weight*] ...]]

where *collating-identifier* is one of the following:

- a single character
- a multi-character element (a one-to-two character code pair or a two-to-one character code pair; see "Collating Sequence" in Chapter 2 for more information)
- an ellipsis symbol
- the special symbol `UNDEFINED`

(Note that *primary-weight* and *secondary-weight* are optional.)

Multi-Character Collating Element

Multi-character collating elements are defined using the `collating-element` keyword. The `collating-element` keyword must be defined prior to the `order_start` keyword using the syntax:

`collating-element` `<`*symbol*`>` `from` `"`*string*`"`

For example, we might want to define a *symbol* as a substitute for a multi-character *string*, which will collate as a single entity, that is, as a two-to-one character code pair, at the point where *symbol* appears in the collating sequence.

The following is an example of `LC_COLLATE` code that defines a collating sequence where the string `C1` collates between the characters `C` and `D`:

```
collating-element   <xx> from "C1"

order_star:
 ...
'C'      'C';'C'
<xx>     <xx>;<xx>
'D'      'D';'D'
 ...
order_end
```

A one-to-two character code pair, consisting of single characters that collate as two adjacent characters, may also be defined. In the following example, the *sharp s* is collated as `ss` and occurs between `S` and `s` in the collation sequence.

```
order_start
 ...
'S'      'S';'S'
\xde     'S';"ss"
's'      'S';'s'
 ...
order_end
```

Ellipsis Symbol

An ellipsis symbol (...) specifies that a sequence of characters collates according to its encoded character values. This means that when an ellipsis is used, all characters with a coded-character-set value greater than the value of the character in the preceding line and less than the coded-character-set value in the following line, will collate in between the two in ascending order, according to their coded-character-set values.

In the following example, the ellipsis indicates that the characters B, C, D, and E (in the ASCII character set) will collate between A and F in the order according to their values in the character set:

```
order_start
'A'  'A';'A'
 ...
'F'  'F';'F'
order_end
```

In this case, the collation order will be A, B, C, D, E, and F. Note that the use of the ellipsis symbol ties the definition to a specific, coded character set such as ASCII or EBCDIC.

`UNDEFINED` Symbol

The symbol `UNDEFINED` is interpreted as "including all coded-character-set values not specified explicitly or via the ellipsis symbol." Such characters, belonging to the character set, but not specified, are inserted in the character collation order at the point indicated by the `UNDEFINED` symbol, and in ascending order according to their coded-character-set values.

In the following example, A to Z will collate before 1 to 9, and all characters not defined (not between A-Z or between 1-9) will collate according to their coded-character-set values, between `Z` and `1`:

```
order_start
'A'  'A';'A'
 ...
'Z'  'Z';'Z'
UNDEFINED
'1'  '1';'1'
 ...
'9'  '9';'9'
order_end
```

Optional Weightings

The optional operands for each collation entry are used to define the primary or secondary weights for the collating element. Two or more elements can be assigned the same primary weight. If so, they are said to be in the same equivalence class. Note that the following two collating-sequence definitions are equivalent:

```
order_start
'A'
'B'
'C'
order_end
```

and:

```
order_start
'A'  'A';'A'
'B'  'B';'B'
'C'  'C';'C'
order_end
```

In the following sample definition, the letters `A` and `a` both belong to the equivalence class `A` and collate before the character `B`. Similarly, the characters `B` and `b` belong to the same equivalence class. However, `a` and `b` collate after `A` and `B` respectively because their secondary weights are different:

```
order_start
'A'   'A';'A'
'a'   'A';'a'
'B'   'B';'B'
'b'   'B';'b'
order_end
```

If the symbol `IGNORE` is used as the secondary weight, it causes the collating element to be ignored during comparisons, as if the string did not contain the collating element.

LC_CTYPE Keywords

When using expressions to classify character types, you can specify character-code ranges by listing two constants defining the range, separated by an ellipsis (...). The constant preceding the ellipsis must have a smaller code value than the constant following the ellipsis. A range represents a set of consecutive character codes.

When using shift expressions, enclose a pair of character codes by left and right parentheses. For **tolower**, the first constant represents an uppercase character and the second the corresponding lowercase character. For **toupper**, the first constant represents a lowercase character, and the second represents the corresponding uppercase character.

The `LC_CTYPE` category consists of the keywords shown in Table 7-5.

Table 7-5. `LC_CTYPE` Keywords

Keyword	Character Code
`upper`	Uppercase letters.
`lower`	Lowercase letters.
`digit`	Numeric characters (0 - 9).
`space`	Spacing (delimiter) characters.
`punct`	Punctuation characters.
`cntrl`	Control characters.
`blank`	Printable space characters. These must also be defined in **`space`**.
`xdigit`	Hexadecimal digits.
`alpha`	Character codes classified as alphabetic characters. If omitted, this class is the concatenation of the **`upper`** and **`lower`** classes.
`print`	Character codes classified as printable characters. If omitted this class is the concatenation of the **`upper`**, **`lower`**, **`alpha`**, **`digit`**, **`xdigit`**, and **`punct`** classes and the **`space`** character.
`graph`	Character codes classified as graphic characters. If omitted, this class is all characters included in the **`print`** class except the **`space`** character.
`first` (HP-specific)	First bytes of two-byte characters.
`second` (HP-specific)	Second bytes of two-byte characters.
`toupper`	Lowercase to uppercase character relationships.
`tolower`	Uppercase to lowercase character relationships.
`charclass`	Character codes specific to a given locale. Note: This keyword is not currently available for users of HP-UX (as of the 9.0 version).

Table 7-5. LC_CTYPE **Keywords (continued)**

Keyword	Character Code
bytes_char (HP-specific)	String containing the maximum number of bytes per character for the character set used for a specific language.
alt_punct (HP-specific)	String mapped into the ASCII equivalent string *b*!"#$%&'()*+,-./:;<=>?@[\]^_'{|}~, where *b* is a blank.
code_scheme (HP-specific)	Specifies the multi-byte character encoding scheme used. The operand should be a string. Currently, HP-15 and EUC are recognized. If this keyword is not specified, or the operand is a null string (""), the encoding scheme is single-byte, or HP-15 if bytes_char is 2.
cswidth (HP-specific)	Defines the number of bytes contained in a character, and the number of columns per character displayed on the output devices. This keyword should be specified if the encoding scheme is EUC.

The following example displays the LC_CTYPE category for the american locale:

```
##########################################################
# Set up the LC_CTYPE category

LC_CTYPE

upper     'A';'B';'C';'D';'E';'F';'G';'H';'I';'J';'K';'L'; \
     'M';'N';'O';'P';'Q';'R';'S';'T';'U';'V';'W';'X'; \
     'Y';'Z';\xa1;\xa2;\xa3;\xa4;\xa5;\xa6;\xa7;\xad;\xae;\xb1; \
     \xb4;\xb6;\xd0;\xd2;\xd3;\xd8;\xda;\xdb;\xdc;\xde;\xdf;\xe0; \
     \xe1;\xe3;\xe5;\xe6;\xe7;\xe8;\xe9;\xeb;\xed;\xee;\xf0

lower     'a';'b';'c';'d';'e';'f';'g';'h';'i';'j';'k';'l'; \
     'm';'n';'o';'p';'q';'r';'s';'t';'u';'v';'w';'x'; \
     'y';'z';\xb2;\xb5;\xb7;\xc0;\xc1;\xc2;\xc3;\xc4;\xc5;\xc6; \
     \xc7;\xc8;\xc9;\xca;\xcb;\xcc;\xcd;\xce;\xcf;\xd1;\xd4;\xd5; \
     \xd6;\xd7;\xd9;\xdd;\xde;\xe2;\xe4;\xea;\xec;\xef;\xf1

alpha     'A';'B';'C';'D';'E';'F';'G';'H';'I';'J';'K';'L'; \
     'M';'N';'O';'P';'Q';'R';'S';'T';'U';'V';'W';'X'; \
```

```
        'Y';'Z';'a';'b';'c';'d';'e';'f';'g';'h';'i';'j'; \
        'k';'l';'m';'n';'o';'p';'q';'r';'s';'t';'u';'v'; \
        'w';'x';'y';'z';\xa1;\xa2;\xa3;\xa4;\xa5;\xa6;\xa7;\xad; \
        \xae;\xb1;\xb2;\xb4;\xb5;\xb6;\xb7;\xc0;\xc1;\xc2;\xc3;\xc4; \
        \xc5;\xc6;\xc7;\xc8;\xc9;\xca;\xcb;\xcc;\xcd;\xce;\xcf;\xd0; \
        \xd1;\xd2;\xd3;\xd4;\xd5;\xd6;\xd7;\xd8;\xd9;\xda;\xdb;\xdc; \
        \xdd;\xde;\xdf;\xe0;\xe1;\xe2;\xe3;\xe4;\xe5;\xe6;\xe7;\xe8; \
        \xe9;\xea;\xeb;\xec;\xed;\xee;\xef;\xf0;\xf1

graph       '!';'"';'#';'$';'%';'&';''';'(';')';'*';'+';',';  \
        '-';'.';'/';'0';'1';'2';'3';'4';'5';'6';'7';'8'; \
        '9';':';';';'<';'=';'>';'?';'@';'A';'B';'C';'D'; \
        'E';'F';'G';'H';'I';'J';'K';'L';'M';'N';'O';'P'; \
        'Q';'R';'S';'T';'U';'V';'W';'X';'Y';'Z';'[';'\'; \
        ']';'^';'_';'`';'a';'b';'c';'d';'e';'f';'g';'h'; \
        'i';'j';'k';'l';'m';'n';'o';'p';'q';'r';'s';'t'; \
        'u';'v';'w';'x';'y';'z';'{';'|';'}';'~';\xa1;\xa2; \
        \xa3;\xa4;\xa5;\xa6;\xa7;\xa8;\xa9;\xaa;\xab;\xac;\xad;\xae; \
        \xaf;\xb0;\xb1;\xb2;\xb3;\xb4;\xb5;\xb6;\xb7;\xb8;\xb9;\xba; \
        \xbb;\xbc;\xbd;\xbe;\xbf;\xc0;\xc1;\xc2;\xc3;\xc4;\xc5;\xc6; \
        \xc7;\xc8;\xc9;\xca;\xcb;\xcc;\xcd;\xce;\xcf;\xd0;\xd1;\xd2; \
        \xd3;\xd4;\xd5;\xd6;\xd7;\xd8;\xd9;\xda;\xdb;\xdc;\xdd;\xde; \
        \xdf;\xe0;\xe1;\xe2;\xe3;\xe4;\xe5;\xe6;\xe7;\xe8;\xe9;\xea; \
        \xeb;\xec;\xed;\xee;\xef;\xf0;\xf1;\xf2;\xf3;\xf4;\xf5;\xf6; \
        \xf7;\xf8;\xf9;\xfa;\xfb;\xfc;\xfd;\xfe

print       ' ';'!';'"';'#';'$';'%';'&';''';'(';')';'*';'+'; \
        ',';'-';'.';'/';'0';'1';'2';'3';'4';'5';'6';'7'; \
        '8';'9';':';';';'<';'=';'>';'?';'@';'A';'B';'C'; \
        'D';'E';'F';'G';'H';'I';'J';'K';'L';'M';'N';'O'; \
        'P';'Q';'R';'S';'T';'U';'V';'W';'X';'Y';'Z';'['; \
        '\';']';'^';'_';'`';'a';'b';'c';'d';'e';'f';'g'; \
        'h';'i';'j';'k';'l';'m';'n';'o';'p';'q';'r';'s'; \
        't';'u';'v';'w';'x';'y';'z';'{';'|';'}';'~';\xa1; \
        \xa2;\xa3;\xa4;\xa5;\xa6;\xa7;\xa8;\xa9;\xaa;\xab;\xac;\xad; \
        \xae;\xaf;\xb0;\xb1;\xb2;\xb3;\xb4;\xb5;\xb6;\xb7;\xb8;\xb9; \
        \xba;\xbb;\xbc;\xbd;\xbe;\xbf;\xc0;\xc1;\xc2;\xc3;\xc4;\xc5; \
        \xc6;\xc7;\xc8;\xc9;\xca;\xcb;\xcc;\xcd;\xce;\xcf;\xd0;\xd1; \
        \xd2;\xd3;\xd4;\xd5;\xd6;\xd7;\xd8;\xd9;\xda;\xdb;\xdc;\xdd; \
        \xde;\xdf;\xe0;\xe1;\xe2;\xe3;\xe4;\xe5;\xe6;\xe7;\xe8;\xe9; \
        \xea;\xeb;\xec;\xed;\xee;\xef;\xf0;\xf1;\xf2;\xf3;\xf4;\xf5; \
        \xf6;\xf7;\xf8;\xf9;\xfa;\xfb;\xfc;\xfd;\xfe

digit       '0';'1';'2';'3';'4';'5';'6';'7';'8';'9'

space       \x9;\xa;\xb;\xc;\xd;' '

punct       '!';'"';'#';'$';'%';'&';''';'(';')';'*';'+';','; \
        '-';'.';'/';':';';';'<';'=';'>';'?';'@';'[';'\'; \
```

```
     ']';'^';'_';'`';'{';'|';'}';'~';\xa8;\xa9;\xaa;\xab; \
     \xac;\xaf;\xb0;\xb3;\xb8;\xb9;\xba;\xbb;\xbc;\xbd;\xbe;\xbf; \
     \xf2;\xf3;\xf4;\xf5;\xf6;\xf7;\xf8;\xf9;\xfa;\xfb;\xfc;\xfd; \
     \xfe

cntrl     \x0;\x1;\x2;\x3;\x4;\x5;\x6;\x7;\x8;\x9;\xa;\xb; \
     \xc;\xd;\xe;\xf;\x10;\x11;\x12;\x13;\x14;\x15;\x16;\x17; \
     \x18;\x19;\x1a;\x1b;\x1c;\x1d;\x1e;\x1f;\x7f;\x80;\x81;\x82; \
     \x83;\x84;\x85;\x86;\x87;\x88;\x89;\x8a;\x8b;\x8c;\x8d;\x8e; \
     \x8f;\x90;\x91;\x92;\x93;\x94;\x95;\x96;\x97;\x98;\x99;\x9a; \
     \x9b;\x9c;\x9d;\x9e;\x9f;\xff

blank     \x9;' '

xdigit    '0';'1';'2';'3';'4';'5';'6';'7';'8';'9';'A';'B'; \
     'C';'D';'E';'F';'a';'b';'c';'d';'e';'f'

toupper   ('a','A');('b','B');('c','C');('d','D'); \
     ('e','E');('f','F');('g','G');('h','H'); \
     ('i','I');('j','J');('k','K');('l','L'); \
     ('m','M');('n','N');('o','O');('p','P'); \
     ('q','Q');('r','R');('s','S');('t','T'); \
     ('u','U');('v','V');('w','W');('x','X'); \
     ('y','Y');('z','Z');(\xb2,\xb1);(\xb5,\xb4); \
     (\xb7,\xb6);(\xc0,\xa2);(\xc1,\xa4);(\xc2,\xdf); \
     (\xc3,\xae);(\xc4,\xe0);(\xc5,\xdc);(\xc6,\xe7); \
     (\xc7,\xed);(\xc8,\xa1);(\xc9,\xa3);(\xca,\xe8); \
     (\xcb,\xad);(\xcc,\xd8);(\xcd,\xa5);(\xce,\xda); \
     (\xcf,\xdb);(\xd1,\xa6);(\xd4,\xd0);(\xd5,\xe5); \
     (\xd6,\xd2);(\xd7,\xd3);(\xd9,\xe6);(\xdd,\xa7); \
     (\xe2,\xe1);(\xe4,\xe3);(\xea,\xe9);(\xec,\xeb); \
     (\xef,\xee);(\xf1,\xf0)

tolower   ('A','a');('B','b');('C','c');('D','d'); \
     ('E','e');('F','f');('G','g');('H','h'); \
     ('I','i');('J','j');('K','k');('L','l'); \
     ('M','m');('N','n');('O','o');('P','p'); \
     ('Q','q');('R','r');('S','s');('T','t'); \
     ('U','u');('V','v');('W','w');('X','x'); \
     ('Y','y');('Z','z');(\xa1,\xc8);(\xa2,\xc0); \
     (\xa3,\xc9);(\xa4,\xc1);(\xa5,\xcd);(\xa6,\xd1); \
     (\xa7,\xdd);(\xad,\xcb);(\xae,\xc3);(\xb1,\xb2); \
     (\xb4,\xb5);(\xb6,\xb7);(\xd0,\xd4);(\xd2,\xd6); \
     (\xd3,\xd7);(\xd8,\xcc);(\xda,\xce);(\xdb,\xcf); \
     (\xdc,\xc5);(\xdf,\xc2);(\xe0,\xc4);(\xe1,\xe2); \
     (\xe3,\xe4);(\xe5,\xd5);(\xe6,\xd9);(\xe7,\xc6); \
     (\xe8,\xca);(\xe9,\xea);(\xeb,\xec);(\xed,\xc7); \
     (\xee,\xef);(\xf0,\xf1)
```

```
bytes_char     "1"
alt_punct ""
code_scheme    ""
cswidth   ""
END LC_CTYPE
```

LC_MESSAGES Keywords

The keywords shown in Table 7-6 are included as part of the LC_MESSAGES category.

Table 7-6. LC_MESSAGES Keywords

Keyword	Function
yesexpr	Expression identifying the affirmative response for yes/no questions.
noexpr	Expression identifying the negative response for yes/no questions.
yesstr	String identifying the affirmative response for yes/no questions. This keyword is now obsolete and **yesexpr** should be used instead.
nostr	String identifying the negative response for yes/no questions. This keyword is now obsolete and **noexpr** should be used instead.

Following is an example for the LC_MESSAGES category:

```
#####################################################

# LC_MESSAGES category

LC_MESSAGES
yesexpr   "^[yY]"
noexpr    "^[nN]"
yesstr    "yes"
nostr     "no"
END LC_MESSAGES
```

LC_MONETARY Keywords

The keywords shown in Table 7-7 are included in the `LC_MONETARY` category.

Table 7-7. `LC_MONETARY` Keywords

Keyword	Description
`int_curr_symbol`	Four-character string specifying the international currency symbol used. The first three characters are alphabetic, specifying the international currency symbol. The fourth character is the character used to separate the international currency symbol from the monetary quantity.
`currency_symbol`	Specifies the currency symbol applicable to the current locale.
`mon_decimal_point`	Specifies the decimal point used to format monetary quantities.
`mon_thousands_sep`	Specifies the separator used to group digits to the left of the decimal point in monetary quantities.
`mon_grouping`	A semicolon-separated list of integers. The initial integer defines the size of the group immediately preceding the decimal delimiter, and the following integers define the preceding groups (`lconv` item).
`positive_sign`	Specifies the character used to indicate positive monetary quantities.
`negative_sign`	Specifies the character used to indicate negative monetary quantities.
`int_frac_digits`	Specifies the number of fractional digits displayed in an internationally formatted quantity.
`frac_digits`	Specifies the number of fractional digits displayed in a locally formatted monetary quantity.

Table 7-7. LC_MONETARY Keywords (continued)

Keyword	Description
`p_cs_precedes`	Specifies if `currency_symbol` precedes or follows a nonnegative formatted monetary quantity. `1` indicates it precedes the value, `0` that it follows it.
`p_sep_by_space`	A value of `1` indicates that the `currency_symbol` or `int_curr_symbol` is separated by a space from a nonnegative formatted monetary value; a value of `0` indicates that it is not. (X/Open, as contrasted to HP-UX, also supports a value of `2` if a space separates the symbol from the string sign.)
`n_cs_precedes`	Specifies if `currency_symbol` precedes or follows a negative formatted monetary quantity. `1` indicates it precedes the value, `0` that it follows it.
`n_sep_by_space`	A value of `1` indicates that the `currency_symbol` or `int_curr_symbol` is separated by a space from a negative formatted monetary value; a value of `0` indicates that it is not. (X/Open, as contrasted to HP-UX, also supports a value of `2` if a space separates the symbol from the string sign.)
`p_sign_posn`	Specifies the string position of the `positive_sign` for a non-negative formatted monetary quantity. **Value:** **Indicates:** `0` Parentheses surround the quantity and currency symbol. `1` The sign string precedes the quantity and currency symbol. `2` The sign string succeeds the quantity and currency symbol. `3` The sign string immediately precedes the currency symbol. `4` The sign string immediately succeeds the currency symbol.

Table 7-7. LC_MONETARY Keywords (continued)

Keyword	Description
n_sign_posn	Specifies the position of the **negative_sign** in a negative formatted monetary quantity. Values indicate the same as for **p_sign_posn** above.
crncystr	Specifies the placement of the currency symbol. If - (minus), it precedes the monetary value, if +, it follows the monetary value, and if ".", it replaces the radix symbol in the monetary value.

The following example displays the LC_MONETARY category for the american locale:

```
####################################################


# LC_MONETARY category

LC_MONETARY
int_curr_symbol      "USD "
currency_symbol      "$"
mon_decimal_point    "."
mon_thousands_sep    ","
mon_grouping   3
positive_sign  ""
negative_sign  "-"
int_frac_digits      2
frac_digits    2
p_cs_precedes  1
p_sep_by_space 0
n_cs_precedes  1
n_sep_by_space 0
p_sign_posn    1
n_sign_posn    1
crncystr  "-US$"
END LC_MONETARY
```

LC_NUMERIC Keywords

The keywords in Table 7-8 are included in the LC_NUMERIC category.

Table 7-8. LC_NUMERIC **Keywords**

grouping	Specifies the number of digits that are grouped together as a unit in formatted non-monetary quantities.
decimal_point	Specifies the radix character used to format non-monetary quantities.
thousands_sep	Specifies the character used to separate groups of digits to the left of the decimal point character in formatted non-monetary quantities.
alt_digit (HP-specific)	Specifies the string mapped into the ASCII equivalent string 0123456789*b*+-.,eE, where *b* is a blank.

The following example displays the LC_NUMERIC category for the american locale:

```
#####################################################
# LC_NUMERIC category


LC_NUMERIC
decimal_point    "."
thousands_sep    ","
grouping         3
alt_digit        ""
END LC_NUMERIC
```

LC_TIME Keywords

The keywords shown in Table 7-9 are defined for the LC_TIME category.

Table 7-9. LC_TIME Keywords

Keyword	Function
d_t_fmt	String specifying date and time format.
d_fmt	String specifying date format.
t_fmt	String specifying time format.
t_fmt_ampm	Time representation in the 12-hour clock format with **am_pm**.
day	Seven semicolon-separated strings giving names for the days of the week beginning with Sunday; they correspond to **nl_langinfo** items **day_1** through **day_7**.
abday	Seven semicolon-separated strings giving abbreviated names for the days of the week beginning with Sunday; they correspond to **nl_langinfo** items **abday_1** through **abday_7**.
mon	Twelve semicolon-separated strings giving names for the months, beginning with January; they correspond to **nl_langinfo** items **mon_1** through **mon_12**.
abmon	Twelve semicolon-separated strings giving abbreviated names for the months, beginning with January; they correspond to **nl_langinfo** items **abmon_1** through **abmon_12**.
am_pm	Two semicolon-separated strings giving the representations for a.m. and p.m.
era	How years are calculated.
alt_digits	Allows for specification of replacement symbols for digits through use of strings separated by semi-colons.
era_d_fmt	Default string for formatting the **%E** (Emperor/Era name and year) directive of *date*(1) and *strftime*(3C) if an individual era format is not specified for an era.
era_t_fmt	Default string for formatting time format.
era_d_t_fmt	Default string for formatting date and time format.

Table 7-9. LC_TIME Keywords (continued)

Keyword	Function
year_unit (HP-specific)	Symbol for years.
mon_unit (HP-specific)	Symbol for month.
day_unit (HP-specific)	Symbol for day.
hour_unit (HP-specific)	Symbol for hour.
min_unit (HP-specific)	Symbol for minute.
sec_unit (HP-specific)	Symbol for second.

Note era, era_t_fmt, era_d_t_fmt, and alt_digits are not currently available for users of HP-UX (as of the 9.0 version).

The following example displays the LC_TIME category for the american locale:

```
#####################################################
# LC_TIME category

LC_TIME
d_t_fmt  "%a, %b %.1d, %Y %I:%M:%S %p"
d_fmt "%a, %b %.1d, %Y"
t_fmt "%I:%M:%S"
t_fmt_ampm "%I:%M:%S %p"

day "Sunday";"Monday";"Tuesday";"Wednesday";"Thursday";"Friday";"Saturday"

abday "Sun";"Mon";"Tue";"Wed";"Thu";"Fri";"Sat"

mon "January";"February";"March";"April";"May";"June"; \
"July";"August";"September";"October";"November";"December"

abmon "Jan";"Feb";"Mar";"Apr";"May";"Jun"; "Jul";"Aug";"Sep"; \
"Oct";"Nov";"Dec"
```

```
am_pm "AM";"PM"

year_unit   ""
mon_unit    ""
day_unit    ""
hour_unit   ""
min_unit    ""
sec_unit    ""
era_d_fmt   ""

END LC_TIME
```

A

Internationalization Routines and Commands

Table A-1 presents an alphabetical listing of standard UNIX internationalization routines and related routines covered in this book along with a description of each.

Table A-1. Internationalization Library Routines

Routine	Description
`asctime`(*const struct tm *timeptr*)	Formats date and time strings returning `C` locale results.
`catclose`(*nl_catd catd*)	Closes message catalog *catd*.
`catgets`(*nl_catd catd, int set_num, int msg_num, const char *def_str*)	Reads message *msg_num* in set *set_num* from the message catalog identified by *catd*, a catalog descriptor returned from a previous call to *catopen*(3C). *def_str* points to a default message string returned by **`catgets`** if the call fails.
`catopen`(*const char *name, int oflag*)	Opens a message catalog and returns a catalog descriptor. *name* specifies the name of the message catalog being opened. *oflag* should be set to **`NL_CAT_LOCALE`**.
`ctime`(*const time_t *timer*)	Formats date and time strings returning `C` locale results.
`fgetc`(*FILE *stream*)	Same as **`getc()`**, but is a function rather than a macro.
`fgets`(*char *s, int n, FILE *stream*)	Reads characters from input into an array.
`fgetwc`(*FILE *stream*)	Returns the next character from the named input *stream*, converts that to the corresponding wide character, and moves the file pointer ahead one character in *stream*. **`fgetwc()`** is defined only as a function.
`fgetws`(*wchar_t *ws, int n, FILE *stream*)	Reads characters from the *stream*, converts them into corresponding wide characters and places them into the array pointed to by *ws*, until *n-1* characters are read, a new-line is read and transferred to *ws*, or an end-of-file condition is encountered. The wide string is then terminated with a null wide character.
`fprintf`(*FILE *stream, const char *format*, `/* [arg,] */ ...`)	Places output in the named output *stream*. Converts, formats, and prints its `[args]` under control of the *format*.

Table A-1. Internationalization Library Routines (continued)

Routine	Description
fputc(*int c, FILE *stream*)	Same as **putc()**, but is a function rather than a macro.
fputs(*const char *s, FILE *stream*)	Writes a string to output.
fputwc(*wint_t wc, FILE stream*)	Writes the character corresponding to the wide character *wc* to the output stream pointed to by *stream*.
fputws(*const wchar_t *ws***,** *FILE *stream***)**	Writes a character string corresponding to the null-terminated, wide character string pointed to by *ws* to the named output *stream*, but does not append a new-line character or a terminating null character.
fscanf(*FILE *stream***,** *const char *format***, /* [pointer,] */** ... **)**	Reads characters from the stream, interprets them according to the control string *format* argument, and stores the results in its **[pointer]** arguments.
getc(*FILE *stream*)	Reads a character from input and converts it to an integer.
getchar(void)	Same as **getc(stdin)**.
gets(*char *s*)	Reads characters from standard input into an array.
getwc(*FILE *stream***)**	Returns the next character from the named input *stream*, converts that to the corresponding wide character, and moves the file pointer ahead one character in *stream*. **getwc()** is defined both as a macro and a function.
getwchar(void)	Is defined as **getwc(stdin)**, so it is both a macro and a function.
iconv(*iconv_t cd, const char **inbuf, size_t *inbytesleft, char **outbuf, size_t *outbytesleft*)	Converts a sequence of characters from one codeset to another codeset.

Table A-1. Internationalization Library Routines (continued)

Routine	Description
`iconv_close(`*iconv_t cd*`)`	Closes the conversion descriptor *cd* and any other resources opened by `iconv_open`.
`iconv_open(`*const char *tocode, const char *fromcode*`)`	Performs necessary initializations for codeset conversions.
`isalnum(`*int c*`)`	Indicates if *c* is alphanumeric (letters or digits). Defined for range -1(EOF) to 255.
`isalpha(`*int c*`)`	Indicates if *c* is a letter. Defined for range -1(EOF) to 255.
`isascii(`*int c*`)`	Indicates if *c* is any ASCII character code between 0 and 0177, inclusive. Defined on all integer values.
`iscntrl(`*int c*`)`	Indicates if *c* is a control character (in ASCII: character codes less than 040 and the delete character (0177)). Defined for range -1(EOF) to 255.
`isdigit(`*int c*`)`	Indicates if *c* is a digit (in ASCII: characters 0-9). Defined for range -1(EOF) to 255.
`isgraph(`*int c*`)`	Indicates if *c* is a visible character. Defined for range -1(EOF) to 255.
`islower(`*int c*`)`	Indicates if *c* is a lowercase alphabetic character. Defined for range -1(EOF) to 255.
`isprint(`*int c*`)`	Indicates if *c* is a printing character. Defined for range -1(EOF) to 255.
`ispunct(`*int c*`)`	Indicates if *c* is a punctuation character (in ASCII: any printing character except the space character (040), digits, and letters). Defined for range -1(EOF) to 255.

Table A-1. Internationalization Library Routines (continued)

Routine	Description
`isspace(`*int c*`)`	Indicates if *c* is a character that creates "white space" in displayed test (in ASCII: space, tab, carriage return, new-line, vertical tab, and form-feed). Defined for range -1(EOF) to 255.
`isupper(`*int c*`)`	Indicates if *c* is an uppercase alphabetic character. Defined -1(EOF) to 255.
`isxdigit(`*int c*`)`	Indicates if *c* is a hexadecimal digit (in ASCII: characters [0-9], [A-F], or [a-f]). Defined for range -1(EOF) to 255.
`iswalnum(`*wint_t wc*`)`	Indicates if *wc* is an alphanumeric (letters or digits).
`iswalpha(`*wint_t wc*`)`	Indicates if *wc* is a letter.
`iswcntrl(`*wint_t wc*`)`	Indicates if *wc* is a control character (in ASCII: character codes less than 040 and the delete character (0177)).
`iswctype(`*wint_t wc*`,`*wctype_t prop*`)`	Indicates if *wc* has the property defined by *prop*.
`iswdigit(`*wint_t wc*`)`	Indicates if *wc* is a decimal digit (in ASCII: characters [0-9]).
`iswgraph(`*wint_t wc*`)`	Indicates if *wc* is a visible character (in ASCII: printing characters, excluding the space character (040)).
`iswlower(`*wint_t wc*`)`	Indicates if *wc* is a lowercase letter.
`iswprint(`*wint_t wc*`)`	Indicates if *wc* is a printing character.
`iswpunct(`*wint_t wc*`)`	Indicates if *wc* is a punctuation character (in ASCII: any printing character except the space character (040), digits, and letters).

Table A-1. Internationalization Library Routines (continued)

Routine	Description
`iswspace(`*wint_t wc*`)`	Indicates if *wc* is a character that creates "white space" in displayed text (in ASCII: space, tab, carriage return, new-line, vertical tab, and form-feed).
`iswupper(`*wint_t wc*`)`	Indicates if *wc* is an uppercase letter.
`iswxdigit(`*wint_t wc*`)`	Indicates if *wc* is a hexadecimal digit (in ASCII: characters [0-9], [A-F], or [a-f]).
`localeconv(void)`	returns locale-specific numeric formatting conventions.
`mblen(`*const char *s*`,` *size_t n*`)`	Determines the number of bytes in the multi-byte character pointed to by *s*.
`mbstowcs(`*wchar_t *pwcs*`,` *const char *s*`,` *size_t n*`)`	Converts a sequence of multi-byte characters from the array pointed to by *s* into a sequence of corresponding codes and stores these codes into the array pointed to by *pwcs*, stopping after either *n* codes or a code with value zero (a converted null character) is stored.
`mbtowc(`*wchar_t *pwc*`,` *const char *s*`,` *size_t n*`)`	Determines the number of bytes in the multi-byte character pointed to by *s*, determines the code for the value of type *wchar_t* corresponding to that multi-byte character, and then stores the result in the object pointed to by *pwc*.
`nl_langinfo(`*nl_item item*`)`	Returns a pointer to a null-terminated string containing information relevant to a particular language or cultural area defined in the program's locale (see *setlocale*(3C)). The manifest constant names and values of *item* are defined in **`langinfo.h`**.
`printf(`*const char *format, /** `[arg,]` **/ ...*`)`	Places output in the standard output *stream*. Converts, formats, and prints its `[args]` under control of the *format*.

Table A-1. Internationalization Library Routines (continued)

Routine	Description
`putc`(*int c, FILE *stream*)	Writes a character to output.
`putchar`(*int c*)	Same as `putc(stdout)`.
`puts`(*const char *s*)	Writes a string to standard output.
`putwc`(*wint_t wc, FILE *stream*)	See `fputwc`.
`putwchar`(*wint_t wc*)	The same as `putwc(wc, stdout)`.
`scanf`(*const char *format, /** `[pointer,]` **/ ...*)	Reads characters from the standard input stream `stdin`. Interprets them according to the control string *format* argument, and stores the results in its `[pointer]` arguments.
`setlocale(`*category*`,` *locale*`)`	Sets the program environment for the specified *category* according to the language definition table for the specified *locale*.
`sprintf(`*char *s*`,`*const char *format*`, /* [arg,] */ ... )`	Places "output", followed by the null character (\0), in consecutive bytes starting at **s*. (It is the user's responsibility to ensure that enough storage is available.) Converts, formats, and prints its `[args]` under control of the *format*.
`sscanf(`*const char *s*`,` *const char *format*`, /* [pointer,]` **/ ...*)	Reads characters from the character string *s*. Interprets them according to the control string *format* argument, and stores the results in its `[pointer]` arguments.
`strcat`(*char *s1, const char *s2*)	Appends a copy of a second string to the end of a first string.
`strchr`(*const char *s, int c*)	Returns a pointer to the first occurrence of a byte in a string, or a null pointer if the byte does not occur in the string.

Table A-1. Internationalization Library Routines (continued)

Routine	Description
strcmp(*const char *s1, const char *s2*)	Returns an integer greater than, equal to, or less than zero, according to whether the first string pointed to is greater than, equal to, or less than the second string pointed to.
strcoll(*const char *s1, const char *s2*)	Compares its two arguments and returns an integer less than, equal to, or greater than zero, depending on whether the first is lexicographically less than, equal to, or greater than the second.
strcpy(*char *s1, const char *s2*)	Copies a second string to a first string, stopping after the null byte has been copied.
strcspn(*const char *s1, const char *s2*)	Returns the length of the maximum initial segment of a first string which consists entirely of bytes not from from a second string.
strfmon(*char *s, size_t maxsize, const char *format*)	Inserts characters into the array pointed to by *s*.
strftime(*char *s, size_t maxsize, const char *format, const struct tm *timeptr*)	Converts contents of a *tm* structure to a formatted date and time string. Places characters into the array pointed to by *s* as controlled by the string pointed to by *format*. No more than *maxsize* characters are placed into the array. The appropriate characters are determined by the program's locale, by the values in the structure pointed to by *timeptr*, and by the **TZ** (time zone) environment variable.
strlen(*const char *s*)	Returns the number of bytes in a string, not including the terminating null byte.
strncat(*char *s1, const char *s2, size_t n*)	Same as **strcat** except appends at most *n* bytes.
strncmp(*const char *s1, const char *s2, size_t n*)	Same as **strcmp** except examines at most *n* bytes.

Table A-1. Internationalization Library Routines (continued)

Routine	Description
strncpy(*char *s1, const char *s2, size_t n*)	Same as **strcpy** except copies exactly *n* bytes.
strpbrk(*const char *s1, const char *s2*)	Returns a pointer to the first occurrence in a string of any byte from a second string, or a null pointer if no byte from the second exists in the string.
strptime(*const char *buf, const char *format, struct tm *tm*)	Converts a time string into a value stored in the time structure. (Opposite operation as **strftime**.)
strrchr(*const char *s, int c*)	Returns a pointer to the last occurrence of a byte in a string, or a null pointer if the byte does not occur in the string.
strspn(*const char *s1, const char *s2*)	Returns the length of the maximum initial segment of a first string which consists entirely of bytes from a second string.
strstr(*const char *s1, const char *s2*)	Returns a pointer to the first occurrence of second string in a first string, or a null pointer if the second string does not occur in the first string.
strtod(*const char *str***,** *char **ptr***)**	Returns, as a double-precision floating-point number, the value represented by the character string pointed to by *str*. The string is scanned (leading white-space characters as defined by **isspace** are ignored) up to the first unrecognized character. If the value of *ptr* is not *(char **)NULL*, the variable to which it points is set to point at the character after the last number, if any, that was recognized. If no number can be formed, **ptr* is set to *str*, and zero is returned.
strtok(*char *s1, const char *s2*)	Considers a string to consist of a sequence of zero or more text tokens separated by spans of one or more bytes from the separator string. The first call returns a pointer to the first byte of the first token, and writes a null byte into the string immediately following the returned token.

Table A-1. Internationalization Library Routines (continued)

Routine	Description
`strtol`(*const char *str, char **ptr, int base*)	Converts the character string pointed to by *str* to `long int` (`unsigned long int`) representation.
`strtoul`(*const char *str, char **ptr, int base*)	Converts the character string pointed to by *str* to `unsigned long int` representation.
`strxfrm(`*char *s1* `,` *const char *s2* `,` *size_t n*`)`	Transforms the string pointed to by *s2* and places the resulting string into the array pointed to by *s1*. The transformation is such that if the `strcmp()` function is applied to two transformed strings, it returns a value greater than, equal to, or less than zero, corresponding to the result of the `strcoll()` function applied to the same two original strings. No more than *n* bytes are placed into the resulting string, including the terminating null character.
`tolower(`*int c*`)` `_tolower(`*int c*`)`	Returns the corresponding lowercase letter if *c* points to an uppercase letter; otherwise returns *c* unaltered.
`toupper(`*int c*`)` `_toupper(`*int c*`)`	Returns the corresponding uppercase letter if *c* points to a lowercase letter; otherwise returns *c* unaltered.
`towlower(`*wint_t wc*`)`	Has as domain a *wint_t*, the value of which is representable as a *wchar_t* or the value `WEOF`. Returns the corresponding lowercase letter if *wc* points to an uppercase letter; otherwise returns *wc* unaltered.
`towupper(`*wint_t wc*`)`	Has as domain a *wint_t*, the value of which is representable as a *wchar_t* or the value `WEOF`. Returns the corresponding uppercase letter if *wc* points to a lowercase letter; otherwise returns *wc* unaltered.
`ungetc`(*int c, FILE *stream*)	Inserts a character into an input stream.
`ungetwc`(*wint_t wc, FILE *stream*)	Pushes the character corresponding to the wide character code *wc* into the buffer associated with an input stream. That wide character code, *wc*, is returned by the next call to `getwc`.

Table A-1. Internationalization Library Routines (continued)

Routine	Description
vfprintf(*FILE *stream, const char *format, va_list ap*)	Same as **fprintf** except called with an argument list.
vprintf(*const char *format, va_list ap*)	Same as **printf** except called with an argument list.
vsprintf(*char *s, const char *format, va_list ap*)	Same as **sprintf** except called with an argument list.
wcscat(*wchar_t *ws1, const wchar_t *ws2*)	Similiar to **strcat** except it appends two wide character strings.
wcschr(*const wchar_t *ws, wint_t wc*)	Similiar to **strchr** except it scans a wide character string.
wcscmp(*const wchar_t *ws1, const wchar_t *ws2*)	Similiar to **strcmp** except it compares two wide character strings.
wcscoll(*const wchar_t *ws1, const wchar_t *ws2*)	Similiar to **strcoll** except it compares two wide character strings.
wcscpy(*wchar_t *ws1, const wchar_t *ws2*)	Similiar to **strcpy** except it copies one wide character string to another.
wcscspn(*const wchar_t *ws1, const wchar_t *ws2*)	Similiar to **strcspn** except it returns the length of a wide character string.
wcsftime(*wchar_t *ws, size_t maxsize, const char *format, const struct tm *timeptr*)	Similiar to **strftime** except it converts the contents of a *tm* structure to a formatted date and time wide character string.
wcslen(*const wchar_t *ws*)	Similiar to **strlen** except it returns the number of wide characters in a wide character string.

Table A-1. Internationalization Library Routines (continued)

Routine	Description
wcsncat(*wchar_t *ws1, const wchar_t *ws2, size_t n*)	Similiar to **strncat** except it appends wide characters.
wcsncmp(*const wchar_t *ws1, const wchar_t *ws2, size_t n*)	Similiar to **strncmp** except it examines wide character strings.
wcsncpy(*wchar_t *ws1, const wchar_t *ws2, size_t n*)	Similiar to **strncpy** except it copies wide character strings.
wcspbrk(*const wchar_t *ws1, const wchar_t *ws2*)	Similiar to **strpbrk** except it returns a pointer to the first occurrence of a wide character in a wide string.
wcsrchr(*const wchar_t *ws, wint_t wc*)	Similiar to **strrchr** except that it returns a pointer to the last occurrence of a wide character in a wide string.
wcsspn(*const wchar_t *ws1, const wchar_t *ws2*)	Similiar to **strspn** except it returns the length of a wide character string.
wcstod(*const wchar_t *nptr, wchar_t **endptr*)	Similiar to **strtod** except it converts a wide character string to a **double**.
wcstok(*wchar_t *ws1, const wchar_t *ws2*)	Similiar to **strtok** except it considers a wide string to consist of a sequence of zero or more text tokens separated by spans of one or more wide characters.
wcstol(*const wchar_t *nptr, wchar_t **endptr, int base*)	Similiar to **strtol** except it converts a wide character string to a **long int**.
wcstombs(*char *s*, *const wchar_t *pwcs*, *size_t n*)	Converts a sequence of codes corresponding to multi-byte characters from the array pointed to by *pwcs* into a sequence of multi-byte characters and stores them into the array pointed to by *s*, stopping if a multi-byte character exceeds the limit of *n* total bytes or if a null character is stored.

Table A-1. Internationalization Library Routines (continued)

Routine	Description
wcstoul(*const wchar_t *nptr, wchar_t **endptr, int base*)	Similiar to **strtoul** except it converts a wide character string to an **unsigned long int**.
wcswcs(*const wchar_t *ws1, const wchar_t *ws2*)	Similiar to **strstr** except it returns a pointer to a wide character.
wcswidth(*const wchar_t *pwcs, size_t n*)	Returns the number of column positions required for a wide character string.
wcsxfrm(*wchar_t *ws1, const wchar_t *ws2, size_t n*)	Transforms the wide character string pointed to by *ws2*, inserting the new string into the array pointed to by *ws1*.
wctomb(*char *s, wchar_t wchar***)**	Determines the number of bytes needed to represent the multi-byte character corresponding to the code whose value is wchar and stores the multi-byte character representation in the array object pointed to by s.
wctype(*const char *charclass*)	Returns a value of type **wctype_t** from a character class name input for use in a subsequent call to **iswctype()**.
wcwidth(*wint_t wc*)	Returns the number of column positions required for the display of a wide character.

Table A-2 presents an alphabetical listing of the standard internationalization commands covered in this book along with a description of each.

Table A-2. Internationalization Commands

Command	Description
`gencat` *catfile msgfile ...*	Generate a formatted message catalog file.
`iconv -f` *fromcode* `-t` *tocode [file ...]*	Codeset conversion command.
`locale [-a|-m] [-ck]` *name ...*	Display current locale environment.
`localedef [-c] [-f` *charmap_file*`] [-i` *input_file] [locale_name]*	Sets up the language environment for a given locale.

Table A-3 presents an alphabetical listing of the HP-specific internationalization routines covered in this book along with a description of each.

Table A-3. HP-UX Internationalization Routines

Routine	Description
`getlocale`*(int type)*	Returns a pointer to a `locale_data` structure. The members of the `locale_data` structure contain information about the setting of each `setlocale` category.
`strord`*(char *s1, const char *s2, nl_mode m)*	Converts the order of characters in *s2* from screen to keyboard order or vice versa and places the result in *s1*. The arguments *s1* and *s2* point to strings (arrays of characters terminated by a null character).

Table A-4 presents an alphabetical listing of the HP-specific internationalization commands covered in this book along with a description of each.

Table A-4. HP-UX Internationalization Commands

Command	Description
`dumpmsg` *file ...*	Extracts messages and set declarations from a message catalog and writes then to standard out.
`findmsg [-a]` *file ...*	Examines C source files and writes to standard output strings embedded in `catgets()` calls and strings tagged with the comment `/* catgets */`
`findstr` *file ...*	Examines C source files for double quoted strings, writing the strings and additional information to standard output; the form of the information is suitable as input to `insertmsg`.
`forder [-a] [-l] [-n]` *[file ...]*	Converts the order of character in a file from screen order to keyboard order or from keyboard order to screen order.
`insertmsg [-h] [-n` *number*`] [-i` *amount]* *[*`-s` *number] stringlist*	Replaces double-quoted strings with `catgets()` calls in a C program source file.
`nljust [-aclnt] [-e` *seq] [*`-j` *just] [*`-m` *mode] [*`-o` *order] [*`-r` *margin] [*`-w` *width] [*`-x` *ck] [file ...]*	Formats data with a right-to-left orientation for printing. (Used with the commands `pr` and `lp`.)

B

Obsolete HP-UX Routines and Interfaces

Obsolete Routines/Interfaces

NLS, Hewlett-Packard's solution to internationalization, is a relatively new technology. As a result of its recent introduction into the UNIX industry and subsequent refinement, NLS is still in the process of development and modification. Industry-wide standards are only beginning to be firmly established, thus there have been different implementations of internationalization.

In keeping with HP-UX's standardization efforts, HP-UX has undergone some changes. Some routines and library interfaces that HP-UX offers are specific to HP-UX. Other internationalization routines/interfaces are specified by different standards (X/Open, POSIX). The HP-UX-specific routines/interfaces are currently supported, but will be withdrawn at some time in the future. Use of the standard routines/interfaces is recommended instead.

Table B-1 lists currently obsolete HP-UX routines/interfaces and their replacements. These routines/interfaces have replacements that provide similar or related functionality. About half of the obsolete routines/interfaces have an equivalent replacement; the only difference is the name of the routine/interface. However, the remaining routines/interfaces do not have an equivalent replacement. Instead, several routines may need to be called or the parameter list may be slightly different.

Table B-1. Obsolete HP-UX Routines and Recommended Replacements

Obsolete Routine	Recommended Routine	Man Page Reference
`buildlang`	`localedef`	*localedef*(1M)
`catgetmsg`	`catgets`	*catgets*(3C)
`catread`	`catgets`	*catgets*(3C)
`currlangid`	*none needed*	
`fprintmsg`	`fprintf`	*printf*(3C)
`getmsg`	`catgets`	*getmsg*(3C)
`ICONV`, `ICONV1`, `ICONV2`	`iconv`	*iconv*(3C)
`iconvclose`	`iconv_close`	*iconv*(3C)
`iconvopen`	`iconv_open`	*iconv*(3C)
`iconvsize`	*none needed*	*iconv*(3C)
`idtolang`	*none needed*	
`langinfo`	`nl_langinfo`	*nl_langinfo*(3C)
`langinit`	`setlocale`	*setlocale*(3C)
`langtoid`	*none needed*	
`msgbuf.h`	*none needed*	
`n-computer`	`C` or `POSIX`	*lang*(5)
`nl_asctime`	`strftime`	*strftime*(3C)

Table B-1. Obsolete HP-UX Routines and Recommended Replacements (continued)

Obsolete Routine	Recommended Routine	Man Page Reference
nl_ascxtime	strftime	*strftime*(3C)
nl_atof	atof	*strtod*(3C)
nl_catopen	catopen	*catopen*(3C)
nl_ctime	strftime	*strftime*(3C)
nl_ctype.h	mbtowc	*multibyte*(3C)
nl_cxtime	strftime	*strftime*(3C)
nl_fprintf	fprintf	*string*(3C)
nl_fscanf	fscanf	*scanf*(3S)
nl_gcvt	gcvt	*ecvt*(3C)
nl_init	setlocale	*setlocale*(3C)
nl_isalnum	isalnum	*ctype*(3C)
nl_isalpha	isalpha	*ctype*(3C)
nl_iscntrl	iscntrl	*ctype*(3C)
nl_isdigit	isdigit	*ctype*(3C)
nl_isgraph	isgraph	*ctype*(3C)
nl_islower	islower	*ctype*(3C)
nl_isprint	isprint	*ctype*(3C)
nl_ispunct	ispunct	*ctype*(3C)

Table B-1.
Obsolete HP-UX Routines and Recommended Replacements (continued)

Obsolete Routine	Recommended Routine	Man Page Reference
nl_isspace	isspace	*ctype*(3C)
nl_isupper	isupper	*ctype*(3C)
nl_isxdigit	isxdigit	*ctype*(3C)
nl_printf	printf	*printf*(3S)
nl_scanf	scanf	*scanf*(3S)
nlsinfo	locale	*locale*(1)
nl_sprintf	sprintf	*printf*(3S)
nl_sscanf	sscanf	*scanf*(3S)
nl_strcmp	strcmp, strcoll	*string*(3C)
nl_strncmp	strncmp, strcoll	*string*(3C)
nl_strtod	strtod	*strtod*(3C)
nl_tolower	tolower	*conv*(3C)
nl_toupper	toupper	*conv*(3C)
printmsg	printf	*printf*(3S)
sprintmsg	sprintf	*printf*(3S)
strcmp8	strcoll	*string*(3C)
strcmp16	strcoll	*string*(3C)
strncmp8	strcoll	*string*(3C)
strncmp16	strcoll	*string*(3C)

Obsolete Multi-Byte Proprietary Interfaces

Data integrity requires that, in processing codeset data, the data must not be corrupted. For single-byte codesets, the eighth bit must be preserved; it must not be stripped or used by the program. For multi-byte codesets, single-byte characters must be correctly distinguished from multi-byte characters.

HP's multi-byte codesets utilize an encoding scheme in which the single-byte character codes for ASCII can be intermixed with the two-byte character codes used to represent ideograms. In these codesets, it is possible for the second byte of a two-byte character to have the same value as an ASCII character.

For an arbitrary byte, it is not possible to know if the byte is a single-byte character or the second byte of a multi-byte character. This is the "byte definition" problem: The second byte of a multi-byte character may be incorrectly interpreted as a one-byte character.

Even for those encoding schemes such as EUC that avoid much of the byte definition problem, an efficient way of dividing a byte stream along character boundaries is needed.

To aid in processing multi-byte codesets and avoid the byte definition problem, there are a number of HP-specific routines available to the programmer.

The 16-bit macros listed below are HP proprietary and are not portable to other vendors' platforms. Therefore, it is recommended that you use the WPI interfaces instead. Information about these interfaces is included to enable programmers to maintain existing applications or port existing applications to the WPI interfaces. The HP-UX `man` page reference for all of these tools is *nl_tools_16*(3C).

Table B-2. Obsolete Multi-Byte Interfaces and Recommended Replacements

Interface Name	Recommended Replacement
ADVANCE	None
BYTE_STATUS	None
byte_status	None
C_COLWIDTH	wcwidth
c_colwidth	wcwidth
CHARADV	mbtowc
CHARAT	mbtowc
FIRSTOF2	None
firstof2	None
PCHAR	wctomb
PCHARADV	wctomb
SECOF2	None
secof2	None
WCHAR	mbtowc
WCHARADV	mbtowc

C

HP-UX Languages and Codesets

Table C-1 shows locale names and native languages currently supported on HP-UX as well as the codesets that support them. Simply find the language (or country) that you are interested in. The HP-specific locale name is shown in the second column.

Note It is recommended that you use the ISO 8859 codesets for new applications or applications that require a high degree of portability. These codesets are based on a widely accepted industry standard.

Codesets in the table that follows that do not begin with the letters ISO are HP proprietary. In most cases, the country-specific codesets correspond exactly to relevant national standards.

Table C-1. HP-UX Language Codesets

lang-id	Locale Name	Language	Codeset
0	n-computer	American English	
101	american.iso88591	American English	ISO 8859-1
1	american	American English	ROMAN8
51	arabic	Arabic	ARABIC8
52	arabic-w	Western Arabic	ARABIC8
301	arabic.iso88596	Arabic	ISO 8859-6
181	bulgarian	Bulgarian	ISO 8859-5
99	C	Computer	
102	c-french.iso88591	French Canadian	ISO 8859-1
2	c-french	French Canadian	ROMAN8
201	chinese-s	Simplified Chinese	PRC15
211	chinese-t	Traditional Chinese	ROC15
212	chinese-t.big5	Traditional Chinese	BIG5
142	czech	Czechoslovakian	ISO 8859-2
103	danish.iso88591	Danish	ISO 8859-1
3	danish	Danish	ROMAN8
104	dutch.iso88591	Dutch	ISO 8859-1
4	dutch	Dutch	ROMAN8
105	english.iso88591	English	ISO 8859-1
5	english	English	ROMAN8
106	finnish.iso88591	Finnish	ISO 8859-1
6	finnish	Finnish	ROMAN8
107	french.iso88591	French	ISO 8859-1
7	french	French	ROMAN8
108	german.iso88591	German	ISO 8859-1
8	german	German	ROMAN8
61	greek	Greek	GREEK8
321	greek.iso88597	Greek	ISO 8859-7
71	hebrew	Hebrew	HEBREW8
341	hebrew.iso88598	Hebrew	ISO 8859-8
143	hungarian	Hungarian	ISO 8859-2

Table C-1. HP-UX Language Codesets (continued)

lang-id	Locale Name	Language	Codeset
114	`icelandic.iso88591`	Icelandic	ISO 8859-1
14	`icelandic`	Icelandic	ROMAN8
109	`italian.iso88591`	Italian	ISO 8859-1
9	`italian`	Italian	ROMAN8
222	`japanese.euc`	Japanese	JAPANEUC
221	`japanese`	Japanese	JAPAN15
41	`katakana`	Katakana	KANA8
231	`korean`	Korean	KOREA15
110	`norwegian.iso88591`	Norwegian	ISO 8859-1
10	`norwegian`	Norwegian	ROMAN8
144	`polish`	Polish	ISO 8859-2
111	`portuguese.iso88591`	Portuguese	ISO 8859-1
11	`portuguese`	Portuguese	ROMAN8
100	`POSIX`	POSIX default	
145	`rumanian`	Rumanian	ISO 8859-2
180	`russian`	Russian	ISO 8859-5
146	`serbocroatian`	Serbo-Croatian	ISO 8859-2
148	`slovene`	Slavic (Slovenia)	ISO 8859-2
112	`spanish.iso88591`	Spanish	ISO 8859-1
12	`spanish`	Spanish	ROMAN8
113	`swedish.iso88591`	Swedish	ISO 8859-1
13	`swedish`	Swedish	ROMAN8
91	`thai`	Thai	THAI8
81	`turkish`	Turkish	TURKISH8
361	`turkish.iso88599`	Turkish	ISO 8859-9

Figure C-1 shows the HP proprietary ROMAN8 coded character set.

				b_8	0	0	0	0	0	0	0	0	1	1	1	1	1	1	1	1
				b_7	0	0	0	0	1	1	1	1	0	0	0	0	1	1	1	1
				b_6	0	0	1	1	0	0	1	1	0	0	1	1	0	0	1	1
				b_5	0	1	0	1	0	1	0	1	0	1	0	1	0	1	0	1
b_4	b_3	b_2	b_1		0	1	2	3	4	5	6	7	8	9	10	11	12	13	14	15
0	0	0	0	0	NUL	DLE	SP	0	@	P	‘	p				¯	â	Å	Á	Þ
0	0	0	1	1	SOH	DC1	!	1	A	Q	a	q			À	Ý	ê	î	Ã	þ
0	0	1	0	2	STX	DC2	"	2	B	R	b	r			Â	ý	ô	Ø	ã	•
0	0	1	1	3	ETX	DC3	#	3	C	S	c	s			È	°	û	Æ	Đ	µ
0	1	0	0	4	EOT	DC4	$	4	D	T	d	t			Ê	Ç	á	å	ð	¶
0	1	0	1	5	ENQ	NAK	%	5	E	U	e	u			Ë	ç	é	í	Í	¾
0	1	1	0	6	ACK	SYN	&	6	F	V	f	v			Î	Ñ	ó	ø	Ì	—
0	1	1	1	7	BEL	ETB	’	7	G	W	g	w			Ï	ñ	ú	æ	Ó	¼
1	0	0	0	8	BS	CAN	(	8	H	X	h	x			´	¡	à	Ä	Ò	½
1	0	0	1	9	HT	EM	)	9	I	Y	i	y			`	¿	è	ì	Õ	ª
1	0	1	0	10	LF	SUB	*	:	J	Z	j	z			ˆ	¤	ò	Ö	õ	º
1	0	1	1	11	VT	ESC	+	;	K	[	k	{			¨	£	ù	Ü	Š	«
1	1	0	0	12	FF	FS	,	<	L	\	l	|			˜	¥	ä	É	š	■
1	1	0	1	13	CR	GS	-	=	M	]	m	}			Ù	§	ë	ï	Ú	»
1	1	1	0	14	SO	RS	.	>	N	^	n	~			Û	ƒ	ö	ß	Ÿ	±
1	1	1	1	15	SI	US	/	?	O	_	o	DEL			₤	¢	ü	Ô	ÿ	

LG200220_007

Figure C-1. HP-UX ROMAN8 Coded Character Set

Figure C-2 shows the standard ISO 8859-1 coded character set.

				b_8	0	0	0	0	0	0	0	0	1	1	1	1	1	1	1	1
				b_7	0	0	0	0	1	1	1	1	0	0	0	0	1	1	1	1
				b_6	0	0	1	1	0	0	1	1	0	0	1	1	0	0	1	1
				b_5	0	1	0	1	0	1	0	1	0	1	0	1	0	1	0	1
b_4	b_3	b_2	b_1		00	01	02	03	04	05	06	07	08	09	10	11	12	13	14	15
0	0	0	0	00			SP	0	@	P	`	p			NBSP	°	À	Ð	à	ð
0	0	0	1	01			!	1	A	Q	a	q			¡	±	Á	Ñ	á	ñ
0	0	1	0	02			"	2	B	R	b	r			¢	²	Â	Ò	â	ò
0	0	1	1	03			#	3	C	S	c	s			£	³	Ã	Ó	ã	ó
0	1	0	0	04			$	4	D	T	d	t			¤	´	Ä	Ô	ä	ô
0	1	0	1	05			%	5	E	U	e	u			¥	µ	Å	Õ	å	õ
0	1	1	0	06			&	6	F	V	f	v			¦	¶	Æ	Ö	æ	ö
0	1	1	1	07			'	7	G	W	g	w			§	·	Ç	×	ç	÷
1	0	0	0	08			(	8	H	X	h	x			¨	¸	È	Ø	è	ø
1	0	0	1	09			)	9	I	Y	i	y			©	¹	É	Ù	é	ù
1	0	1	0	10			*	:	J	Z	j	z			ª	º	Ê	Ú	ê	ú
1	0	1	1	11			+	;	K	[	k	{			«	»	Ë	Û	ë	û
1	1	0	0	12			,	<	L	\	l	|			¬	¼	Ì	Ü	ì	ü
1	1	0	1	13			-	=	M	]	m	}			SHY	½	Í	Ý	í	ý
1	1	1	0	14			.	>	N	^	n	~			®	¾	Î	Þ	î	þ
1	1	1	1	15			/	?	O	_	o				¯	¿	Ï	ß	ï	ÿ

LG200220_008

Figure C-2. ISO 8859-1 Coded Character Set

Note

On a HP-UX system, you can display a table of supported one-byte characters on a particular device by directing the output of the following program to that device:

```
#include <stdio.h>
main()
{
   int c1,c2,pchar;
   printf("  \\  0  1  2  3  4  5  6  7  8  9 10 11 12 13 14 15\n");
      for (c1=0; c1<16; c1++){
         printf("%3d  ",c1);
         for (c2=0; c2<16; c2++){
            pchar=(((c2*16+c1)&0x7f)>31)?(c2*16+c1):' ';
            printf("%c  ",pchar);
         }
         printf("\n");
   }
}
```

Glossary

ASCII

Acronym for American Standard Code for Information Interchange. ASCII is a 128-character codeset represented by 7-bit binary values. (ASCII does not define the value of the eighth bit.) Also, referred to as USASCII.

bit

A contraction of binary digit. A bit can have a value of 0 or 1.

byte

A unit of data storage consisting of 8 bits. A byte represents one 8-bit character.

C locale

The standard or default language environment on POSIX compliant systems. This environment is always in effect for non-internationalized applications or when language tables (locales) are not installed or are not requested by a program.

character

A series of one or more bytes representing a single graphic symbol or control code.

character set

See **codeset**.

codeset

Unambiguous rules establishing a one-to-one relationship between each character of a set of characters and its corresponding bit and byte representation. *See also* **7-bit codeset**, **8-bit codeset**, **single-byte codeset**, and **multi-byte codeset**.

collating sequence
The ordering sequence assigned to characters or a group of characters when they are sorted and ordered by a computer.

data directionality
Refers to the direction that a language is read by its readers, and by consequence, the direction text from that language will appear on a terminal screen, left-to-right or right-to-left.

data integrity
Maintaining characters as originally input without corrupting the content of the characters.

directionality
See **data directionality**.

downshifting
The conversion of an uppercase character to its lowercase representation.

eight-bit (8-bit) codeset
A codeset that uses all eight bits of a single byte to encode each character in the codeset. These codesets are designed so the range 0 through 127 are nearly always identical to the ASCII codeset. Non-ASCII characters appear in the range 128 through 255. Western European languages are often represented with 8-bit codesets. Examples are the ISO-8859-1 and ROMAN8 codesets.

encoding scheme
A set of rules for interpreting a byte stream as a group of characters.

Extended Unix Code (EUC)
An encoding scheme defined by AT&T USO Pacific to support multi-byte character sets. EUC comprises a primary codeset (CS0) which is 7-bit ASCII, and three supplementary codesets (CS1 through CS3) that can be any character set that the user chooses. These codesets are distinguished by the high bit of the code and the single-shift characters (SS2 and SS3).

HP-15
An HP-proprietary encoding scheme for multi-byte coded character sets. It

is used to represent Traditional Chinese, Simplified Chinese, Korean, and Japanese.

HP-16

An HP-proprietary encoding scheme for multi-byte codesets used for communicating 8- and 16-bit data between a peripheral and a computer.

HP-UX

Hewlett-Packard's proprietary implementation of UNIX.

ideograph

A symbol used to represent an object or an idea.

internationalization

The design and modification of software by developers to allow it to have the capability to be consistent with the language and culture of the geographic areas in which it will be used. Software that has been internationalized can be adapted to the needs of those who speak, read, or write various languages. It can also be adapted to various local customs and coded character sets.

ISO

An international standards organization.

ISO 10646-1

A recently developed character set standard that encodes a set of characters large enough to support most modern languages as well as several specialized applications.

ISO 8859-1

ISO-defined 8-bit single-byte codeset for certain Latin-based alphabets used for most Western European languages and in many North and South American languages. Based on Part 1 of the ISO 8859 International Standard.

ISO 8859-2

ISO-defined 8-bit single-byte codeset used in many Eastern European countries. Based on Part 2 of the ISO 8859 International Standard.

language table
See **locale**.

locale
That part of a computer user's environment which contains specific information relevant to a specific language and/or geographic region, such as collating sequence, time, date, and monetary formatting information, etc. Also called language table.

localizable software
Software that results from the internationalization effort. Such software does not have to be re-coded or re-designed to meet the needs of international users.

localization
The process of adapting an existing software product for use in a particular country or geographic region. Localization activities are usually performed by users of internationalized software, system administrators, and translators.

message catalog
A file external to a program's source code containing the program's messages, prompts, and responses to prompts. The use of a message catalog enables the program to be written in a language-independent fashion but still able to retrieve information appropriate to a given locality.

mode
The order in which text is displayed: Latin (left-to-right), or non-Latin (right-to-left).

multi-byte character
A character represented by two or more bytes as opposed to a single byte only.

multi-byte codeset
A codeset that uses two or more bytes to encode characters. Languages such as Chinese, Japanese, and Korean require more than 256 characters, the maximum provided by eight-bit single-byte codesets.

Native Language Input/Output (NLIO)

An HP-UX subsystem consisting of utilities and libraries designed to support input and output for Asian languages.

Native Language Support (NLS)

A feature of Hewlett-Packard's implementation of UNIX (HP-UX) that provides the software developer with tools to develop internationalized software and the user with localizable software. NLS was subsequently adopted and further modified by X/Open as part of industry-wide and worldwide standard UNIX.

one-to-two character code pair

The practice in some languages of expanding a single character when sorting it and treating it as if it were really two characters.

order

Refers to the temporal order in which data is used. Can be either keyboard order (the order in which the user enters keystrokes) or screen order (the order in which characters are displayed). Will be primarily of relevance only for internationalized programs to be displayed in non-Latin languages, such as Arabic and Hebrew.

POSIX

Acronym for Portable Operating System Interface for Computer Environment. This represents standards for UNIX prescribed by the IEEE. C programming language interface standards are defined in POSIX.1. Shell language standards are defined in POSIX.2.

POSIX locale

See **C locale**.

radix character

The actual or implied character that separates the integer portion of a number from the fractional portion.

regular expression

A string of characters representing a set of matching strings, used in detecting text patterns.

ROMAN8
The HP-proprietary 8-bit codeset for Western European languages.

seven-bit (7-bit) codeset
A codeset that uses seven bits of a single byte to represent each character in the codeset. A 7-bit codeset allows a maximum of 128 characters and therefore cannot accommodate international languages. ASCII is an example of a 7-bit codeset.

Shift JIS
A de facto standardized encoding scheme for the Japanese language, especially for PCs.

single-byte character
A character represented by 7 or 8 bits only (one byte) as opposed to more than one byte.

single-byte codeset
A codeset that represents characters with 7-bit or 8-bit characters only as opposed to multi-byte codesets.

two-to-one character code pair
The practice in some languages of pairing two characters and treating them as a single character before sorting them.

UNICODE
A consortium concerned with developing a universal codeset. Also refers to the character set defined by this consortium.

upshifting
The conversion of a lowercase character to its uppercase representation.

USASCII
See **ASCII**.

wide character
A data object of type `wchar_t` that is large enough to represent any character regardless of the codeset from which it is derived.

Worldwide Portability Interfaces (WPI)

Functions which allow programmers to create applications which support either single-byte or multi-byte codesets. WPI functions are similar to the C language interface but use "wide characters." (*See* **wide character** for more information.)

X/Open

An international organization dedicated to establishing a standardized, or open, UNIX environment.

Index

D

E

F

N

O

P

X

Y